Blend, but Don't Break

A Planning Guide for Blending New Stepfamilies

Mat Singer

Cover designed by Mat Singer & DSP Cover Creator
Cover image used under license from Shutterstock.com
Editing contributions from Liz Coursen and Gretchen Scherer

This book is a work of non-fiction. Names, characters, places, and incidents either are products of the author's imagination or are used fictitiously. Any resemblance to actual persons, living or dead, events, or locales is entirely coincidental.

Mat Singer
Visit my website at www.blendbutdontbreak.com

Printed in the United States of America

First Printing: Feb 2018
Arcola Enterprises LLC

ISBN 9781977015259

I dedicate this to MacKenzie, Cheney, and Kael for enduring many difficult blended family experiences. To Raleigh for being my courageous partner through our childhood blended family challenges and for your never-ending love and support. To Penny for a lifetime of accepting us as your children, not step-children. To Tami for your love and for openly sharing many difficult experiences to add rich context to this book. To many of my friends who shared your experiences, difficulties and feedback to help me craft this book.

Two people in love, want to live as but one
A daughter, a puppy and probably a son

Intentions are golden and goals are pure
Hope is brimming and purpose is sure

More than a few obstacles, before you await
Ground rules to set before the first gate

Richness of bonding and rewards of love
Purposes profound and goals up above

A family is priceless, much effort it will take
Plan and prepare so you blend, but don't break

CONTENTS

CHAPTER 1: INTRODUCTION

Intrigue, excitement and a few butterflies
Her smile, that hair, those beautiful eyes

A date, one weekend, a roadtrip, then vacation
Same food, common hobbies, even my station

Flirt, kiss, date, like, then love
Fits like those jeans, fave sweater or a worn-in glove

Sleepover, housemate, couple drawers, bathroom sink to fend
Can I, should I, will I ask her to blend

Welcome, and thank you for taking the time to learn about ways to enable you to have a more healthy, happy blended family! The book title is based on the American football adage "Bend but Don't Break", which is a familiar term used for a defensive strategy that intends to yield some yards to the opponent, but never give up the big play. In simpler terms, you can give a little along the way, but it leads to ultimately winning the game. Also, the defense's commitment, high skill level and alignment to this strategy are critical to achieving success. This book turns those principles into a framework and process for couples considering blending a family. My definition of a blended family is when two partners choose to live together in an arrangement where one or both partners brings a child or multiple children from a prior relationship into the home. One or both partners will become a stepparent and one or both partners will be moving into a new residence.

I wrote this book shortly after failing spectacularly at my first attempt at blending a family. I moved into a new home that included me, my girlfriend, my three children and eventually a large dog. My girlfriend was a first-time step-parent in training. I freely admit that I think I made every mistake possible over a three-and-a-half-year period of living in a blended family. We were both functional, intelligent, well-intentioned people that could not find it within ourselves to make it work. We tried numerous counselors, support groups, online articles and books. However, we didn't realize that our philosophical gaps were too wide and our own communication styles were too misaligned to allow the relationship to survive. It turned out to be much more emotionally and intellectually complex than either of us could have imagined. After three and a half years of living together, the relationship ended in a blur of fury, anger, contempt, sadness and relief.

I am also the product of multi-blended family childhood. Dad married twice more after he and my mother divorced. The first re-marriage involved just a new step-mom and the second involved a new step-mom and a step-brother. My mom remarried once and that marriage resulted in a new step-dad and three step-siblings. If you're keeping score, I am up to four blended family experiences as a child and adult and have experienced two step-mothers, a step-father, three step-brothers and one step-sister. If you add in my biological sister, quite a few poodles, a couple cats and a small lizard, I've had quite the extended family. While I hadn't previously had a need to reflect on the sheer magnitude of the chaos and complexity my childhood and adult family life entailed, writing this book has certainly opened that window into the past to help me retrieve experiences and examples that have proven very useful for context and stories.

As I look back on my life, I have definitely wondered why there were so many marriages and subsequent divorces. As it turns out, my parents were much like millions of other adults trying a second or even a third marriage. One source, KSL.com, quotes, "The bad news is less than one-third of these (second/ third marriages) new families will last. The divorce rate for second marriages, when only one partner has children, is over 65 percent. When both partners have children, the rate rises to 70 percent and the divorce rate for third marriages is 73 percent." As Captain Obvious would point out, those are shockingly poor odds! I contend that a significant contributor to those failure rates is the tendency for couples to create new blended families with little to no preparation. Personally, I've likened a blended family relationship to climbing Mt Everest while solving physics problems. Would you ever just show up on the first basecamp with no preparation and planning? Imagine how vulnerable and scared you would feel part-way up the journey when you realized that you didn't know the right path, didn't have the right tools, and were highly stressed due to the magnitude of your journey ahead. There is extreme physical, intellectual and emotional complexity involved in maintaining the right path, monitoring the needs of your body at such high altitudes and calculating every footstep and ice axe plant. Those who plan thoroughly, train extremely hard and prepare meticulously have the best chance to summit Everest. Given the second/third marriage odds cited above, you should put a new blended family somewhere in the same ballpark as a Mt Everest challenge. It will take years of hard work and determination to be successful. It will be a significant financial investment and it will come with many intellectual and emotional challenges. You can reach the summit, like Everest, but if you don't plan for all of those elements, your odds of success are going to be very slim.

There's a funny scene in the movie *Dumb and Dumber* when Lloyd Christmas, one of the main "dumb" characters, is flirting with an attractive woman he has quite a crush on. Finally, she tells Loyd that his chances with her are about one in a million. Rather than accepting defeat, Lloyd enthusiastically exclaims, "So you're saying there's a chance. YEAH!" I encourage you to develop a similar optimism about the success of your blended family because you're going to be much better prepared after reading this book. If you understand the obstacles and you prepare to get around them, you have a great chance to overcome the odds and have a happy blended family. Trust me, your odds will be much better than one in a million!

You should also be prepared to face the harsh reality that perhaps your current or potential blended family relationship isn't going to work out. The success rate for summiting Mt. Everest is about 50%. The fact is that even the most well-informed, well-funded, well-prepared people don't always reach a goal that involves such complexity and variability in circumstances, and you can bet that the odds of success are vastly lower without all the preparation and planning. Many people do all the hard work, spend a great deal of money, arrive at one of the basecamps and never make it any further. The trade-off to that disappointment is you're avoiding something much worse. In the case of a mountain climber, you're most likely avoiding death or serious harm. In the case of two people contemplating a blended family, you're avoiding emotional trauma and pain. You're going to avoid a degree of financial hardship that follows separating households, moving, finding new housing, etc. You're also avoiding the unproductivity and unhappiness that comes along with any serious relationship break-up. Now, add in the emotional impact to the children, and you can see the stakes are very high!

The goal of this book is to help couples contemplating or actively planning a blended family understand the building blocks necessary to have a successful family and give you guidance on things you can work on to continue to make the relationship healthy and happy. If you are in the midst of a blended family situation, this will help you too. You're probably reading this because you're experiencing challenges and need guidance on how to address them. This book will be very useful for those purposes as well!

PA.W.S.

My building blocks for a successful blended family are philosophical alignment, will and skill. Let's dig into each one to provide a thorough understanding of how they factor into your blended family.

The first ingredient for blended family success is *philosophical alignment*. Let's start with the definition.

> *Philosophical Alignment = Achievement of an understanding of another's core beliefs, truths, and principles and assessment of where you fit relative to those beliefs, truths, and principles*

One definition of philosophy is the study of the fundamental nature of knowledge, reality, and existence. We don't need to be quite so esoteric in our definition. We just need to understand what it means to figure out where on the spectrum each partner is on core blended family issues. You don't have to understand the philosophy behind why one partner wants a teenage curfew to be 9pm and the other doesn't want any curfew at all. You just need to understand that there is a difference and how big that difference is to each partner. In many relationships, the couple shrugs off the difference of opinion about the curfew and doesn't worry about it at all. In other relationships, there's a two-hour screaming match after Jody, the sixteen-year-old, asked to stay out until midnight with her friends and one parent agreed without input from the other. All partners in a relationship have beliefs about house rules, parenting styles, finances and more. You need to seek out how you each philosophically align on these core topics and assess the degree of misalignment. What you may find is that all the commitment, best intentions and investment in relationship best practices may not overcome vastly different philosophies about raising children, running a household, or spending money.

I want to discuss skill next because the connection between skill and will makes more sense in this order. Also, the acronym PA.S.W. makes no sense and is not cute, so after this section you can stick to remembering PA.W.S. and all will be good. Let's start with the definition of skill and go from there.

> *Skill = the ability, coming from one's knowledge, practice, aptitude, etc., to do something well*

As a child I had a fleeting fantasy of becoming a professional basketball player. I really loved the game and played organized basketball from about 3rd grade on. I went to the gym to practice, played pickup games, did drills to improve my shooting and dribbling, and worked out to increase my speed and vertical jump. I worked harder than just about anyone on my team or at my school. The big problem that I just couldn't escape was the fact that I really didn't have much skill and my potential to be great was quite limited. This 6'1" Anglo (that means white kid) was not ordained at birth with much natural ability and building my skill didn't come easy. I had a huge work ethic and was athletically above average, but I couldn't dribble all that well and couldn't really shoot worth a darn. I did the drills and learned the technique, but I just honestly didn't have a fraction of the natural gifts that someone like Steph Curry had. Steph hit the genetic lottery. His father was Dell Curry, a long-time player for the Charlotte Hornets and several other teams, who had a deadly three-point shooting touch. When you watch Steph shoot compared to his father, you can see the remarkable similarity. How is it possible that a father can pass on three-point shooting skill? Is shooting skill a genetic trait? My non-scientific answer is that the ability to shoot a three pointer isn't a genetic trait. What Steph did inherit from his mom and dad was a body and mind that allowed him to develop into one of the greatest basketball players from our era. His potential was off the charts. Steph was on a professional basketball court as soon as he could walk. He had a lifetime coach (Dell) that was one of the best three-point shooters of his time. Throw in influence and guidance from other NBA players and coaches with genetic physical gifts, and you have a Steph Curry that was a dominant player at a young age. In high school, Steph was all-conference, all-state, and led his team to three conference titles and three state playoff appearances (wikipedia.) Steph had undeniable physical gifts, but it was how he channeled his expert-level guidance and how he spent his time practicing that took raw talent and turned it into skill.

We are all born with physical, intellectual and emotional potential. Your parents and ancestors endowed you with these gifts but they didn't include the instruction manual to know what they are or what to do with them. Most of us muddle through childhood without understanding where we might be gifted and where our potential might be particularly low. In hindsight, I look back and think that my physical attributes were going to cap my potential as a basketball player. I invested a great deal to develop my skill so I could maximize my potential, but no matter how hard I tried, I was never going to become a professional basketball player. If I had truly understood my physical potential, I could have focused on a different sport that better leveraged my physical capabilities and potentially could have been truly great. Steph had fantastic potential as a basketball player, and he and his parents figured out a way to maximize it so he could become a stand-out player.

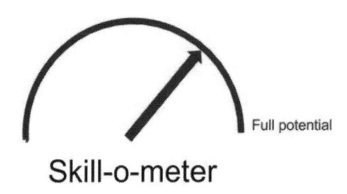

So how does *skill* apply to the traits and attributes someone possesses to be in a successful relationship? Did Dell and Sonya Curry also give Steph the genetic gift of great communication skills, empathy, and humility? The answer is not quite. Just like you and I, Steph genetically inherited intellectual and emotional potential. Our parents, friends, family members, teachers, and others contributed to the development of our intellectual and our emotional skills so we could interact and function in our environment. We rarely think of our childhood games on the playground, interactions with siblings, discussions with parents or lectures from teachers as helping us reach our emotional or intellectual potential. It all just amounts to our experiences throughout our childhood years that shapes our ability to have relationships, converse with people, relate at work and raise our children. We aren't nearly as conscientious about developing our emotional potential as we are our intellectual potential. In the United States, most school curriculums are focused on teaching a balance of academic subjects that will allow us to function in a profession. They aren't focused on how to help us have healthy relationships or be skillful communicators outside of work. This lack of developing our skills as we're emotionally maturing makes it even that much more important to invest in the next key to success in a blended family: or -- *will*.

> *Will = determination or intention to complete or accomplish something*

We explored the fact that Steph Curry won the genetic lottery and had one of the best basketball coaches (dad) to develop his skill from a very young age. However, great genes and the best advice ever still doesn't translate into mastery or expertise in anything. While Steph was following his Dad around the country, he also witnessed the work ethic, discipline and commitment that it took to use that skill to become great. The NBA season is a long grind, so longevity and success weren't just about working hard on the court. Professional athletes have to work very hard during practice, watch video to scout the other team, maintain their diet and work hard in the weight room. Their full-time job is to physically and mentally prepare for winning. The actual game is just a byproduct of everything leading up to the first whistle. Steph never could have turned his high school career success into such accolades and recognition in college if he didn't continue to increase commitment, dedication and focus on becoming the best. Steph did translate those lessons into a storied college career at Davidson University. He was AP All-American Second Team, was named Most Outstanding Player of the Midwest Region of the 2008 NCAA tournament and was nominated for an ESPY award from ESPN. That work ethic, determination and commitment, all amounts to tremendous will.

In the context of a blended family, success demands on will just as much as anything else. Your commitment to the relationship and the success of the family is paramount because you will face deeply personal challenges regarding how you parent your children, how you think a step-child should be parented, how money is spent on the family and household and so many more. You can't shrivel when faced with these challenges while building your family. You have to demonstrate consistent, extensive determination to get through emotionally complex situations. You have to show your partner and the children that your commitment will help you and them get through difficulties.

APPLICATION OF PA.W.S.

Now let's put PA.W.S. together and apply it fully to the context of a blended family. Here are the three questions that you and your partner will seek answers to as you explore your potential for a successful blended family.

1. Are you philosophically aligned on common core issues most blended families will face or at least have a clear appreciation for each partner's stance on the core blended family issues?
2. Do you each possess the will to develop those skills and/or overcome philosophical gaps?
3. Do you each have enough of the skills required to build a blended family relationship and handle the pending complexity?

You really need a healthy dose of all three to give your new family the best chance for success. However, it's important to appreciate that different mixes of each three can point toward a greater or lesser chance of success. For example, if one or both partners have a low skill level at communicating, but have strong will to learn and improve and have high philosophical alignment, you've got a great chance! You may have never learned the basics of communication between couples, but you are darn determined and open-minded to do so. You've also found that you both believe in showing empathy, compassion and love whenever discussing difficult topics. That's great philosophical alignment on one key principle of successful relationships:

Low skill + strong will + medium philosophical alignment = ☺

If one or both partners have high skill and a strong will but medium philosophical alignment, you've got a chance! In this case, both partners are well-versed in different communication techniques and have very strong intention to keep improving. However, you find yourselves debating about the right way to communicate to children because you were both raised by parents who had somewhat different communication styles. Thankfully, you aren't too far off with your beliefs about communication style, so you have several excellent ingredients for success.

> *High skill + strong will + medium philosophical alignment = ☺*

If your <u>will</u> and <u>philosophical alignment</u> are both very low, you're going to need to dig deep to find the will or you face long odds to be successful. For example, Manuel believes that household spending should be strictly according to a budget and he can't see any other way to spend. He is mostly immovable on this topic because he was raised by an accountant and strict financial discipline was ingrained at an early age. Maria believes that each partner should spend according to their income. She doesn't want to be constrained by a tight budget. She works hard and doesn't want overbearing financial oversight and she's not really willing to bend. In this case, both partners have low will and don't have much philosophical alignment. Not being able to connect on a core family issue like this tends to lead to frustration, arguments, stress and larger relationship issues. Couples needs to appreciate that being inflexible on core issues is not an ingredient for success. You have to be willing to be flexible and try to overcome your gaps or you decrease your odds of success.

> *Med/ high skill + low will + no philosophical alignment =☹*

Story: Jessica and Rob moved in together after dating for six months. Rob had no children while Jessica brought three kids ranging from 7-12 from a prior relationship. Early on in their new blended family relationship they encountered a massive challenge -- cupboards. You see, Rob simply wanted the kids to close the cupboard doors after getting food from the pantry or a glass from the cabinet. Rob could not understand why the kids couldn't remember such a simple task and he couldn't understand why Jessica wasn't more active in enforcing this rule. At first, when he brought it up to Jessica, she didn't view it as something very important, so she shrugged off the discussions as Rob nitpicking. Her <u>will</u> to address that issue given so many other important things to focus on was low. In fact, she could really care less about whether the cupboard doors were open or closed. She actually saw Rob leave them open himself sometimes. Her philosophy about what was important to focus on when raising the kids was quite opposite of Rob's. Rob believed that rules should be set, rules should be followed, and kids should have consequences if the rules aren't followed. This issue festered over time such that Rob would actually get enraged when he saw the cupboard doors left open. He focused that rage on the kids and Jessica. How in the world could something so small lead to yelling?! The cupboard issue became emblematic of how they dealt with many house rules and differences of opinion about disciplining the children. Before they moved in together, Rob and Jessica didn't discuss their beliefs about how the home should be maintained and didn't find common ground on how the children should be disciplined if rules were broken. They also didn't establish expectations for what was appropriate communication rules. Rob and Jessica made it about five years before their communication gaps and philosophical differences with the children and house rules tore apart their relationship. The marriage ended in a fiery, expensive mess that ultimately required several visits from the police, a prolonged divorce proceeding, plenty of hard feelings and numerous emotional bruises on the kids.

WHEN TO BEND

As previously explained, the defensive strategy of "bend but don't break" relies on an intentional defensive alignment of players to yield small plays to the opposing team offense with the goal of never giving up any big plays. We want to apply this concept of "giving a little, but winning in the end" to both your blended family relationship and the process you will go through in this book. In this book, you will intentionally be guided through assessments of your philosophical alignment, skill and will, and you will find some topics that are sensitive, difficult to discuss, and will cause disagreement with your partner. The objective is to explore them with your partner at a depth that is otherwise difficult to reach during normal interactions. It is also an objective to address these topics prior to living together so you can assess whether you possess the right combination of PA.W.S. to make the relationship work. As you progress through these assessments and start to negotiate with your partner to find alignment on core blended family topics, be thinking about how you can bend and compromise. There will be topics that are particularly emotional for you, like household finances, and topics that are emotional for your partner, like parenting style. Be prepared to achieve common ground on how you both can appreciate each other's viewpoint, and strategize how you two as a couple will deal with those situations when you're living together.

COMMUNICATION IS KING, EMPATHY IS QUEEN

One last point that I want to stress before we dive in. Let's talk about the table stakes for getting through this book. "Table stakes" refers to the minimum bet required if you're going to play a hand of poker. In this case, the table stakes are the minimum skills you and your partner must possess to get through this book. The first table stake is having the capacity to communicate. The phrase "communication is king" is essentially saying that the most important thing is communication. It particularly applies in the context of this book. If you or your partner don't have solid communication skills, you're going to struggle discussing the topics in this book, and you're going to seriously struggle in your blended family relationship. If there's one thing I've learned, poor communication = poor relationship. You will find out very quickly that when you're addressing topics that are personal and sensitive to one partner or the other, strong communication skills will help you negotiate that topic. If you don't have them, prepare for battle. You're in for many contentious discussions. Let's hope you're not a spitter or stomper during arguments. Those are the worst.

I don't actually know where the cliche' "communication is king" came from, but I felt like it was about time it had a companion. Thus "empathy is queen" was born. The next most important skill you need to bring to this blended family party is empathy. We will explore this further in a later chapter, so if you're unclear on whether you or your partner have any empathy, I'll help you assess that later. The main point is you must express understanding and caring for your partner as you explore topics in this book. You both need to be vulnerable and you both need to feel safe being vulnerable in your discussions. If you're the type that will go ballistic when a cupboard door is open, hope your partner can show you empathy while you explain your point of view, so you both find understanding, not criticism and judgment.

Time to get started, so settle in and enjoy your journey to a better future!

CHAPTER 2: WHY BLEND?

Socks, towels, books and shoes
Crayons, cups, papers and glues

Open, arrange, tidy or fold
Praise, encourage, enforce or scold

Curfew, dinner, homework and dress
Great, blah or enough to impress

Their hearts and their minds and not just lids
So many priorities when it comes to the kids

Answering the question of why live together and blend families might seem intuitive, but it's really not straightforward. I believe that most partners have more than one motive in mind and that's perfectly fine. The point of this book is to be a guide, so you'll be challenged to clarify your intentions and discuss them with your partner. As mentioned earlier, communication is THE most essential ingredient, so I'm going to highly encourage that communication take place well in advance of starting the blending.

WHY MOVE IN TOGETHER?

Let's start with the question as your first exercise. **Write down your reasons for wanting to move in together.** Try to avoid simple answers like, "because I'm in love." Challenge yourself to come up with all the reasons. There's no shame in calling out the potential financial benefit or wanting to be less lonely. Be honest and use this as an opportunity to open up more to your partner.

Partner A

Partner B

Your next step is to spend time talking to your partner about your answers. Are you aligned or off-base with your responses? It's ok to have different motives, but this could be your first opportunity to avoid a challenging blended family relationship if you're far off on your reasons.

Story: Brenda and Tom had been dating for about a year when the topic of getting married and living together came up in conversation. Brenda was three years from a divorce and was raising two kids in an urban apartment on a minimum wage income. Tom was a successful psychiatrist who also divorced and had three children. Brenda and Tom had a close connection and were in love. However, the prospect of getting married and living together had very different implications for each of them. Brenda was seeking stability and security for her and her kids. She really struggled to provide basic comforts for herself and the kids and was constantly tired from working hard and tending to the kids at night. Tom was financially secure and wasn't particularly overworked. The demands of his job were more emotional than physical. However, Tom was lonely at night and didn't like being by himself much. He was looking to regain a little of that happy family companionship he used to have before his first marriage went bad. He wanted a family to travel and share adventures with. If you had asked these two why they wanted to get married again, surely it would have been for all the right reasons; love, commitment, etc. The truth is there was much more behind their motives that would eventually impact their ability to stay married. Tom and Brenda struggled to agree on how to discipline the kids and that disagreement often turned into bitter arguments. They argued often about how he treated his children differently when they visited and how he had a double-standard for punishment of his children vs. hers. The security and lifestyle she sought was replaced with conflict and fear. The loving family he was looking for turned into feeling alienated within his own home. After five years, Brenda and Tom went through their second divorce and five children witnessed their first blended family break-up.

POTENTIAL CONCERNS

The next question to pose to each other is what are your concerns about blending your families? If you have a long list of concerns, don't worry! You should have a few questions and a little trepidation. It's a big step and shouldn't be taken lightly. This list can be used as your framework to build plans to deal with each partner's concerns. Later, you'll have a chance to address these concerns in a structured manner.

Partner A

Partner B

List of potential concerns to get you started:
- Will I lose my free time?
- It might be complicated to figure out expenses for the new home
- I'm not sure I can live with your kids
- Will our kids get along?
- I'm not sure if I should be paying for your kids
- I don't want someone else disciplining my children
- It will be complicated figuring out when my/ your parents visit
- Will your parents and relatives like me or the kids?
- This could affect child support or alimony/ spousal maintenance

- I don't know if I can live with how neat/ messy you/ your kids are
- I am worried about your pets
- I am worried about our pets getting along
- I don't want to give up my time with my friends
- I don't know what to do with my existing home
- I'm not used to living with kids and have no idea what to expect
- The noise of children or pets gives me fear or anxiety
- I don't want your friends in our home
- I am concerned about your use of alcohol or drugs around the kids
- I am concerned about you smoking in the home or around the kids

CHILDREN

If the children involved in your blended family are old enough, let's get them involved in the fun. Ask the child(ren) to identify a few of their concerns or questions about joining a blended family. You will be pleasantly surprised how much better your kids will adapt to a new blended family if they are part of the process and can share their concerns, feelings, and excitement. They could become THE biggest factor in the success of the blended family, so don't ignore them in the process.

List of potential questions or concerns:
- How will bedrooms be chosen?
- Will bedrooms have to be shared?
- What will it be like to live with new pets?
- What will my other parent think if I live with a new parent?
- Is it ok to like or love my new stepparent?
- What will it be like to live with new siblings?
- Will I have to share my things with my new siblings?
- Will I have to change schools?
- Will I have to stop seeing my other parent or see him/ her less?

- Can I decorate my room?
- Will I be able to get a new pet?
- I don't want to follow someone else's rules
- Will I have to follow the new parent's rules?

Story: Rashad and Monique moved in together and each brought a child from their first marriage. Rashad's son, Malik, was 10 and Monique's daughter, Nia, was 12. Rashad and Monique agreed that Rashad's large dog, Bucket, would be part of the new family, but they never asked Monique's daughter Nia how she felt about it. Nia would interact with the dog whenever they visited Rashad's house, but secretly she was grossed out by the dog and didn't like it touching her. After they moved in together Rashad and Malik were continually saying how great Bucket was, how fun and lovable he was and how much better the new home was since Bucket was there. Nobody ever gave Nia a chance to voice her concerns, express her opinion or have the time to create her own opinion of whether she liked Bucket in the home. Nia grew to really dislike interacting with the dog and voiced her displeasure whenever the dog approached her, licked her or jumped on her. She was mad that everyone kept telling her how she should feel about the dog and she was mad about the dog always invading her space. Rashad took Nia's complaints about the dog personally and increased how much he complimented the dog. That interaction eventually turned into sarcastic comments about the dog and Rashad. Nia started to dislike Rashad because he pushed that dang dog on her so often. If only Rashad and Monique had included both kids in conversations about how to build their new family, respected their input and given them time to establish their own opinions about the important factors, such as the dog, they might have had more success.

WHAT EXCITES YOU?

To end this exercise on a positive note, **write down several things that excite you and the children about your new blended family**. Take a little time to share your thoughts with your partner and have fun planning a future together.

Story: One of the benefits of my blended family home was that the home my partner and I purchased had an in-ground swimming pool. We had plenty of access to pools at nearby rec centers, but having a pool in the backyard was a very appealing feature to us and the children. The kids certainly had trepidation about moving out of our existing home, but a feature like a pool created excitement and optimism about the new arrangement. I talked to the kids about the home before we purchased it, showed them pictures, and took them for a walk-through before we made the offer. By the time we moved in, they were really jazzed about it. It made the difficult moving process in June much better because they knew a few hot, sweaty days of moving would be followed by many fun days of lounging in the pool! Getting them excited about our new blended family home really helped ease the trepidation and fear of moving into a new house with a new future step-parent.

FAMILY GOALS

If you want extra credit, each of you write down a few goals you have for your blended family. Think about specific practical goals (ie. family dinner twice per week, all chores complete at the end of the day for a month) or more subjective (i.e. no arguments, everyone says "I love you" before bed, the kids build a positive relationship with the new stepparent).

Examples of goals:

- Family meetings once per week to discuss any issues or concerns with the new family
- Family dinner every Sunday night to share experiences
- The kids spend one night per month on a "date" with the new parent to get to bond with them better
- All concerns from the kids are written down and shared on the whiteboard
- The family will adopt a set of house rules within 30 days of moving in
- House rule review every three or six months
- Nobody holds back feelings or concerns about the new blended family--sharing and communicating is mandatory

Story: A friend of mine, John, shared his experience of contemplating moving in with his girlfriend, Ellen, and her two sons. His child was grown and out of the house, so he would potentially be the only one moving into a well-established home where everyone understood the rules but him. Not to mention, Ellen's sons were teenagers. Through the course of dating and spending time at the home, John had already established that he was not completely aligned with Ellen about house rules and parenting style. He was raised with different beliefs and had established habits and ideas while he was raising his daughter. While he was just there for a few hours at a time, it wasn't a big deal for him to suppress his different ideas how to deal with various situations. However, when the conversation with Ellen turned to the possibility of moving in, he was actually terrified. He had no idea how he would be able to find common ground with all three of them on so many issues. Ultimately, he elected not to move in until the boys were grown and out of the house. John and Ellen are married now and enjoying deep happiness together. The boys live out of state, and now John gets to enjoy them as young men and friends and avoided all the potential conflict that could have (would have) occurred had he moved in.

CHAPTER 3: BLENDED FAMILY SKILLS

Hindsight is a blessing
An insight worth confessing

Potential is an ever reach
Lessons we must learn and teach

Was there enough effort on my quest?
Can I say I did my best?

Did I truly try to fulfil?
Each of those most useful skill

As I reflected on my lessons learned from growing up in blended families and attempting one of my own, I was able to identify several keys to success. These are the inherent *skills* or traits you and your partner currently possess based on how each of you were raised and your accumulation of education and life experiences. As you go through this chapter, you should think about both your current skill level and your ability or *willingness* to explore and expand the skills that may not be developed yet. The intent is that you and your partner can identify your strengths and weaknesses with these skills and then use the resources referenced (or a few of your own) to improve those that are most valuable to your blended family's success.

I realize this list won't be all-encompassing. Every encounter where I have the opportunity to discuss blended family success stories or difficulties, I learn more about what it takes to make them successful. My hope is that this book lives beyond version one and I'll be able to leverage feedback from my readers to collect many other keys to success.

SKILL 1 - COMMUNICATION

As I already explained, communication skills will be extremely important to getting the most of this book. Communication is the foundation of relationships and certainly the foundation of a blended family. Even if you have self-identified as someone with "good" communication skills, there's a decent chance you haven't contemplated what your communication style is. It's definitely worth taking the time to evaluate what your style is so you can assess how that fits with the style of your partner. If your relationship prior to blending has been mostly confrontation-free and you haven't had a chance to stress-test your communication style interaction, I highly recommend you explore this carefully so you don't discover after you've blended your family that your styles are highly uncomplimentary. Just because you have strong communication skills doesn't mean you will mesh will with those of your partner.

There are MANY different frameworks and models out there to define communication styles. One style published in *Forbes* by best-selling author Mark Murphy suggested the four communication styles are Analytical, Intuitive, Functional and Personal. **Analytical** is described as "an Analytical communicator, you like hard data, real numbers, and you tend to be suspicious of people who aren't in command of the facts and data." (Yes, that's me for sure. While discussing topics, I need data and not subjective interpretation. This doesn't work well with people who want to discuss and debate with emotion and generalities.) In contrast, an **Intuitive** communicator is described by "you like the big picture, you avoid getting bogged down in details, and you cut right to the chase." (I cringe when debating any meaningful topic with these types.) If you are an Analytical communicator and your partner is Intuitive, imagine how challenging it might be to come to common ground about an issue with one of the children having to do with grades. The analytical communicator wants to see the assignments and attendance and evaluate the trend over time. The intuitive communicator just wants to understand the factors that may affecting the child's performance. Appreciating where each are coming from is essential to ending up on common ground.

The **Functional** communicator prefers to speak with specificity. You want to understand details, the process, when something will occur, what the plans are and how it fits on the calendar. Being highly detail oriented can be a huge advantage, however if you're trying to agree on something like household finances with an Intuitive communicator, you are likely to experience frustration. If two Functional communicators are discussing household finances, you'll probably end up with a detailed spreadsheet, a budget, a three-year forecast and savings goals for the children.

The **Emotional** communicator wants to establish a connection with the other person so he/ she can discover what they're thinking and feeling. They are very good listeners and tend to develop deep relationships. When dealing with a new step-child's behavior issues, they'll tend to want to understand why the child is feeling the way they are and want to connect with them emotionally. The Analytical communicator would be assessing how egregious the non-compliance was before assessing an appropriate consequence. They care less about what the child is thinking and feeling and more about what consequence will correct the behavior. The conversation between these two could be challenging because the Analytical person wants a solution and the Emotional communicator wants to understand the emotions behind the actions. The Emotional communicator is coming from a place of empathy; whereas, the Analytical communicator is assessing and evaluating the facts and most likely not attempting to share empathy with his/ her partner or the child.

Whether you identify with the Murphy communication style or one of the many other communication frameworks available, it will still be helpful to perform a self-assessment. This will greatly help you and your partner understand where each other is from a PA.W.S. standpoint and give you indicators on where to focus improvement efforts.

As a couple, take the opportunity to self-rate how you view different aspects of your communication style.

My Murphy communication style is:

	Partner A	**Partner B**
Analytical		
Intuitive		
Functional		
Emotional		
It depends on the topic		

My capacity to discuss relationship and family issues is:

	Partner A	**Partner B**
I always have difficulty expressing myself		
A few topics are naturally easy to discuss, others are difficult for me		
I'm comfortable talking about all topics but may need a little help to get started		
I'm willing to share my views whenever asked		
I share my opinions and can discuss anything without reservation		
Everybody always knows exactly what's on my mind		
Other (explain)		

My prior experience and education learning and developing communication skills is:

	Partner A	Partner B
No prior education, self-taught		
Read a book or couple of articles, but otherwise pretty limited formal education		
Attended at least one seminar/ workshop and read several books and articles		
Formal education (college classes) and significant self-study or guided workshops		
Educated enough to teach the class		
An expert on the topic either through formal education or extensive experience		
Other (explain)		

My receptivity to getting professional guidance to develop communication skills:

	Partner A	Partner B
Not open to seeing a counselor, therapist or attend couples' workshops		
Willing to consider it, but need convincing		
Willing to seek professional guidance but only in private settings		
Open to the idea, let's give it a try		
A little prior experience already, big proponent of professional guidance		
Gung ho, let's do it all if it will help		
Other (explain)		

My willingness to involve the children in establishing our blended family rules (if applicable age):

	Partner A	Partner B
The child(ren) should not be involved at all		
It's the parent's job to create rules, only involve the kids selectively		
Open to it but need to figure out what's appropriate		
Decent lines of communication with the child(ren) but let's expand it		
I already include them in everything, let's continue		
Other		

Now that you've gone through the assessment, design a plan to address any gaps or differences that need to be explored further or require additional discussion.

Topics to Discuss

Action Plans

Steps we will take to address the topics, issues or challenges we identified in the section above.

Online Resources

If you'd like to explore communication styles further, check out one of these resources.

1) Which of These Communication Styles Are You? By Mark Murphy
https://www.forbes.com/sites/markmurphy/2015/08/06/which-of-these-4-communication-styles-are-you/2/#7f70738e54ea

2) The Five Communication Styles: http://www.clairenewton.co.za/my-articles/the-five-communication-styles.html

3) Are We Talking the Same Language? How Communication Styles Can Affect Relationships https://www.psychologytoday.com/blog/high-octane-women/201104/are-we-talking-the-same-language-how-communication-styles-can-affect

4) Communication Style Self-Assessment: http://www.newlineideas.com/communication-style-quiz.html

5) Quiz: What's Your Communication Style? http://www.leadershipiq.com/blogs/leadershipiq/39841409-quiz-whats-your-communication-style

6) What's My Communication Style? http://www.hrdqstore.com/communication-style.html

Books

1) Nonviolent Communication: A Language of Life by Marshall B. Rosenberg and Arun Gandhi

2) The Art of Communicating by Thich Nhat Hanh

3) Crucial Conversations Tools for Talking When Stakes Are High by Kerry Patterson and Joseph Grenny

4) Communication Miracles for Couples: Easy and Effective Tools to Create More Love and Less Conflict by Jonathan Robinson

5) How to Talk to Anyone: 92 Little Tricks for Big Success in Relationships by Leil Lowndes

SKILL 2 - PATIENCE

There's a nice quote I found that sums up this key, "Our human tendency is to be impatient with the person who cannot see the truth that is so plain to us. We must be careful that our impatience is not interpreted as condemnation or rejection." This is so poignant to me because I might literally register zero on the patience scale some days. Patience must be a virtue when you are discussing challenging issues as you plan your blended family. It must be present when you are confronted with situations with your partner when you're new to blending your families. Most importantly, it's vital when you're dealing with your children or new blended family children. Children require extreme patience extremely often!

If you need help becoming more patient, the good news is there are many resources available. The guiding tenant you should follow is patience takes practice. Once you learn a few of the tactics, you can practice and become more patient.

Let's see where you and your partner fall on the scale of patience.

My patience level dealing with everyday circumstances is:

	Partner A	Partner B
Little to no patience with most things big and small		
Only impatient when there's a schedule		
Impatient for a few things and not others, depends		
Usually patient under all but abnormal circumstances		
Always patient and relaxed		
Other (explain)		

My patience level when dealing with intense relationship issues is:

	Partner A	Partner B
Immediately walk away most occasions		
Easily frustrated and quick to react		
Usually able to listen to my partner's perspective without reacting		
Stable and sturdy, I can be calm and patient as long as it takes		
Other (explain)		

My patience level dealing with issues with the child(ren) is:

	Partner A	Partner B
I have none		
It's very limited		
Pretty solid but can get worn down over time		
Middle of the road level of patience		
Very patient		
Saintly amount of patience		
Other (explain)		

My receptivity to learning more about patience and developing this attribute:

	Partner A	Partner B
Zero		
Reluctant but convincible		
Open to spending a little time on this		
Open to it but let's discuss		
Fully committed, let's make it happen		
Other (explain)		

Now that you've gone through the assessment, design a plan to address any gaps or differences that need to be explored further or require additional discussion.

Topics to Discuss

Action Plans

Steps we will take to address the topics, issues or challenges we identified in the section above.

Online resources

1) How To Be Patient: https://www.mindtools.com/pages/article/newTCS_78.htm
2) Article: http://www.huffingtonpost.com/2014/09/19/patience-tips_n_5843928.html
3) WikiHow http://www.wikihow.com/Be-Patient
4) Psychology Today https://www.psychologytoday.com/blog/your-zesty-self/201109/four-steps-developing-patience
5) Code of Living http://www.codeofliving.com/life/how-to-be-more-patient-in-control-of-your-life/

Books

1) Patience by Daniel Clowes
2) Patience: The Art of Peaceful Living by Allan Lokos
3) How to Be More Patient: An Essential Guide to Replacing Impatience with Patience by Greg Souchester
4) The Power of Patience: How This Old-Fashioned Virtue Can Improve Your Life by M.J. Ryan
5) Healing Anger: The Power of Patience from a Buddhist Perspective by Dalai Lama and Thupten Jinpa

SKILL 3 - LOVE

One might think this is an obvious ingredient to success for a relationship of any sort, much less a blended family relationship. However, there are a couple unique angles to examine that will help you understand why love is a unique element of blended family success.

The first angle has to do with your reasons for blending a family in the first place. Let's face it, sometimes couples decide to move in together for reasons other than love. It could be to share living expenses, could be out of necessity, convenience or good intentions to eventually become a loving relationship. When love isn't strong between the two partners, it can be much more challenging to face conflict in a unified way. Both partners may not be patient and empathetic with the other's viewpoint and that can grow into destructive behavior. Love can be the potent antidote to conflict, but if it's not present or not strong, then two partners faced with adversity must have several other tools to effectively deal with it.

The second angle relating to love has to do with contending with the biological bond that parents have with their children. If you're working through any challenge with children involved in a blended family, you will encounter emotions in your partner that are fueled by his/her biological bond with their children. That biological need to protect and shield your children can often get in the way of logic and reason. That basis is one of the reasons why love for your partner is so important to success in a blended family. You will face issues that are deeply personal and emotional to the partner that has biological children, and your love must be very strong to help you endure working through those challenging issues.

Story: Another friend I interviewed shared with me that her experience as a married woman in a blended family was very positive, for the most part. I reflect on one key thing she mentioned about how they reacted whenever there was a disagreement about something to do with the ex-husband, her child, or a related topic. She said that she always felt really bad when she got in a disagreement because it hurt her to disappoint or anger her husband. Her love for him was so strong that it really affected her if they had a disagreement. She felt that it equally affected him as well. That deep love helped them quickly reconcile the differences that arose and it remains one of the most important factors in their ongoing happiness. The continue to have a happy, healthy blended family today.

Now that you've gone through the assessment, determine a plan to address any gaps or differences that need to be explored further or require additional discussion.

Topics to Discuss

| |
| |
| |
| |
| |

Action Plans

Steps we will take to address the topics, issues, or challenges we identified in the section above.

Online Resources

1) 10 Ways to Have Peaceful, Loving Relationships http://tinybuddha.com/featured/10-ways-to-have-peaceful-loving-relationships/

2) What is love and a good relationship? http://www.baggagereclaim.co.uk/what-is-love-and-a-good-relationship/

3) 12 Real Signs of True Love in a Relationship http://www.lovepanky.com/love-couch/romantic-love/signs-of-true-love-in-a-relationship

4) If You Do These 10 Things You're Headed Toward Lasting Love (Yay!) http://www.yourtango.com/experts/dr-lynda-klau/top-10-tips-building-loving-relationships-expert

5) Relationship advice: five experts reveal the secrets to long-term love http://www.telegraph.co.uk/women/sex/relationship-advice-and-romance/11016984/Relationship-advice-five-experts-reveal-the-secrets-to-long-term-love.html

Books

1) Me without You by Ralph Lazar and Lisa Swerling

2) The 5 Love Languages: The Secret to Love that Lasts
by Gary Chapman

3) How to Love (Mindful Essentials) by Thich Nhat Hanh and Jason DeAntonis

4) What I Love About You by Kate Marshall and David Marshall

5) The Mastery of Love: A Practical Guide to the Art of Relationship: A Toltec Wisdom Book
by Don Miguel Ruiz and Janet Mills

SKILL 4 - EMPATHY

Empathy is the ability to understand and share the feelings of others. This key is so important because it demonstrates that you have the capacity to be patient, listen, and understand your partner's point of view. You have the ability to put yourself in his/ her "shoes" and see something from his/ her perspective. Coming to common ground or negotiating a compromise must entail both partners having empathy for one another. I firmly believe that empathy is an innate characteristic of people <u>and </u>a skill that can be practiced and developed. Some people have a naturally high empathy quotient and demonstrate an ability to relate very well to other people and understand their emotions and point of view. Others can practice skills like active listening and discussing emotions to better understand how another is feeling.

If you find that you could use a little practice developing more empathy, check out the resources below.

My view of my personal level of empathy is:

	Partner A	Partner B
None		
It's in there but hard to demonstrate		
Strong empathy but doesn't always come out at the right times		
Able to express it most occasions		
The empathy tap is always flowing		
Other		

My receptivity to learning more about empathy and developing this attribute:

	Partner A	Partner B
Zero		
Reluctant but convincible		
Open to spending a little time on this		
Open to it but let's discuss		
Fully committed, let's make it happen		
Other (explain)		

Rate your view of importance to success of a blended family:

	Partner A	Partner B
Rating (1=low, 10=high)		

Now that you've gone through the assessment, figure out a plan to address any gaps or differences that need to be explored further or require additional discussion.

Topics to Discuss

Action Plans

Some steps we will take to address the topics, issues, or challenges we identified in the section above.

Online Resources

1) Power of Empathy http://psychcentral.com/blog/archives/2014/06/08/the-power-of-empathy-in-romantic-relationships-how-to-enhance-it/

2) Learn to Be More Empathetic https://www.psychologytoday.com/blog/making-change/201411/want-better-relationships-learn-be-more-empathic

3) Seven Ways Empathy Can Improve Your Relationship http://www.chatelaine.com/health/sex-and-relationships/seven-ways-empathy-can-improve-your-relationship/

4) How To Practice Empathy http://www.counselling-directory.org.uk/counsellor-articles/how-to-practice-empathy-in-relationships

5) What to do When Your Partner Lacks Empathy http://margaretpaul.com/relationships/what-to-do-when-your-partner-lacks-empathy

Books

1) Empathy: Why It Matters, and How to Get It by Roman Krznaric

2) The Art of Empathy: A Complete Guide to Life's Most Essential Skill by Karla McLaren

3) Born for Love: Why Empathy Is Essential--and Endangered by Bruce D. Perry and Maia Szalavitz

4) Mirroring People: The Science of Empathy and How We Connect with Others by Marco Iacoboni

5) Empathy by Ker Dukey

SKILL 5 - HUMILITY

Humility is freedom from pride or arrogance or the state of being humble. As you plan your blended family, you'll encounter numerous topics that could be considered deal-breakers to you. For example, punishment style for your biological children. Humility is such an essential ingredient as you approach these types of issues because you don't want to end up letting your pride to be right or get your way dominate your true intention, to create a happy blended family.

We are all products of how we were parented and because of that and many other factors, we come into a blended family relationship with many strong preconceived notions. If you think you're always right because you were raised a certain way, you're going to really need to work on being humble and opening yourself up to other styles and ideas. The reality is there is no single right way to have a successful relationship, raise kids or blend a family. There are an infinite number of variations and the only thing you need to worry about is figuring out what combination of variables works for you, your partner, and the kids.

My final point on this key is you must also know when to put your pride aside and ask for help. You may have issues from your past or have issues you are facing at present that you and your partner simply can't negotiate. Go find resources online or seek professional guidance to help you solve your problem. If you are too prideful to see a counselor or therapist, you are further limiting your opportunity for long-term success. Face it, we all have a little baggage and issues that are highly complex. When you bring those into a nuclear engineering complex blended family situation, you're occasionally going to need a lifeline from a qualified resource.

My personal level of humility is:

	Partner A	Partner B
None		
It's in there but hard to demonstrate		
Strong but doesn't always come out at the right times		
Able to express it most occasions		
The tap is always flowing		
Other (explain)		

My personal level of humility is:

My receptivity to learning more about humility and developing this attribute:

	Partner A	Partner B
Zero		
Reluctant but convincible		
Open to spending a little time on this		
Open to it but let's discuss		
Fully committed, let's make it happen		
Other (explain)		

Rate your view of importance to success of a blended family:

	Partner A	Partner B
Rating (1=low, 10=high)		

Now that you've gone through the assessment, figure out a plan to address any gaps or differences that need to be explored further or require additional discussion.

Topics to Discuss

Action Plans

Some steps we will take to address the topics, issues or challenges we identified in the section above.

Online Resources

1) Egos To The Left, To The Left: The Importance Of Being Humble When In Love
   http://madamenoire.com/347115/humility-love-2/

2) Humility Goes a Long Way in a Relationship
   https://psychcentral.com/blog/archives/2016/03/08/humility-goes-a-long-way-in-a-relationship/

3) The Importance Of Humility In Relationships
   http://www.badassyoungmen.com/humility-in-relationships.html

4) Being humble can help your love life http://www.chicagotribune.com/lifestyles/sc-fam-0707-humility-relationships-20150625-story.html

5) Why relationships can't work without Humility.
   https://thelovemanifesto.wordpress.com/2012/12/29/why-relationships-cant-work-without-humility/

Books

1. The Power of Humility: Choosing Peace over Conflict in Relationships by Charles L. Whitfield and Barbara H. Whitfield

2. The Power of Humility: The Secret to Being Happy
   by Mr. Clay J Mize

3. Humility: the neglected Key: Humility by Ruth Dickson

4. Pride In Contrast To Humility by Francis Okweda

5. Humbling and Humility: Small Print Edition by Rian Nejar

SKILL 6 - ARGUMENT AVOIDANCE

It's very important to appreciate that not every issue can be solved in a single discussion or argument. My experience has been that the harder and longer you try to resolve a complex, emotional issue, the worse off you are. You can try hard and take your time, but grinding over something in a single setting is rarely productive. When your body starts to show physical stress from an argument and your brain starts moving from rational thought to instinctual thought, you're most likely moving from discussion to argument. A simple guideline is to take 30 min to discuss a topic. Notice I said "discuss" and not argue. If you can't come up with a resolution or compromise, put it on the shelf for 30 min or come back to it later in the day or the next day. Considering writing down your position on the topic during your break so you can articulate yourself more clearly when you're ready to come back together. That should help you keep your rational brain focused on the topic rather than letting your emotions interfere.

If you or your partner have a tendency to quickly get into argument mode, cut your discussions off quickly. Once either of you are starting to use one of the Four Horsemen (contempt, criticism, defensiveness, stonewalling) then you're not apt to come to a happy conclusion. Take a break and get back to a place where you're able to discuss and compromise. If this is a challenge area for you and your partner, spend a little time looking at these resources. I also highly recommend contacting a counselor who can help you both develop better techniques to avoid arguing.

My tendency to argue:

	Partner A	Partner B
No ability to avoid it, it's built in to who I am		
Quick argument trigger. I'm going to argue my point often		
I'll only argue certain points, situationally dependent		
Infrequent at most		
Arguing is not in my nature at all		
Other (explain)		

My receptivity to developing this skill:

	Partner A	Partner B
Zero		
Reluctant but convincible		
Open to spending a little time on this		
Open to it but let's discuss how much		
Fully committed, let's make it happen		
Other (explain)		

Rate your view of importance to success of a blended family:

	Partner A	Partner B
Rating (1=low, 10=high)		

Now that you've gone through the assessment, design a plan to address any gaps or differences that need to be explored further or require additional discussion.

Topics to Discuss

Action Plans

Some steps we will take to address the topics, issues or challenges we identified in the section above.

Online Resources

1) How a Little Space and Time Can Help Heal a Relationship Crisis
   http://psychcentral.com/blog/archives/2014/08/28/how-a-little-space-and-time-can-help-heal-a-relationship-crisis/

2) Top 10 Tools to Avoid Ugly Arguments
   https://www.psychologytoday.com/blog/emotional-fitness/200908/top-10-tools-avoid-ugly-arguments

3) How to Prevent Arguments
   https://www.psychologytoday.com/blog/blamestorming/201411/how-prevent-arguments

4) Stop Fighting! 4 Ways To Avoid An Argument
   http://www.yourtango.com/experts/christine-brondyke/how-avoid-argument

5) Three Awesome Ways to Avoid an Argument
   http://www.selfgrowth.com/articles/Briggs15.html

Books

1) Everybody Wins: The Chapman Guide to Solving Conflicts without Arguing (Chapman Guides) by Gary Chapman

2) Arguing Constructively by Dominic A. Infante

3) Breaking the Argument Cycle: How To Stop Fighting Without Therapy by Sharon Rivkin

4) The Lost Art of Listening, Second Edition: How Learning to Listen Can Improve Relationships by Michael P. Nichols PhD and Sean Runnette

5) Why Don't We Listen Better? Communicating & Connecting in Relationships by James C. Petersen and Anita Jones

Story: I recall a story from a friend about his and his partner's approach to arguing. Early in their blended family relationship, they found themselves having prolonged arguments about parenting and house-related topics. Neither partner had particularly savvy skills with discussing contentious topics, so they would just spar on simple topics for an hour or more. After months of burning a lot of emotional and physical energy, they went to see a counselor and were able to establish a few ground rules when disputes arose. The counselor advised them to engage in a disputed topic for no more than five minutes at a time. If the conversation became argumentative, then they were to take a ten or fifteen-minute break. If they couldn't resolve it the second time, then they were to take another break, but they had to write down what they would be willing to compromise to find a solution. After a third time, they had to give it a day and come back to it. My friend said it took trial and error to learn how to stop the argument at five minutes, but it was a successful tool to avoid minor issues from escalating. When you add up all the various things that will come up throughout a blended family relationship, you have to realize that both parties will have to compromise numerous times to maintain a peaceful, happy home. Taking these little breaks and identifying where you are able to compromise helps you keep your rational mind in charge of the situation. You can get to the place where you are willing to compromise because you know you'll want your partner to compromise on another issue.

SKILL 7 - COMPROMISE

A quote I liked about compromise comes from Donna Martini, a noted health and wellness advocate. It says, "Compromise is not about losing. It's about deciding that the other person has just as much right to be happy with the end result as you do." When you start to discuss the topics in the "guide" section of this book, compromise is going to have to be one of your sharpest and most available tools y. It's highly unlikely that you and your partner are going to have the same values, philosophies, life experiences or opinions that will be the basis for how you want to build your blended family. You are both going to have to compromise extensively if you want to create a peaceful set of rules and guidelines to live by.

The foundation for compromise is built with your willingness to want to make your new blended family work and your own innate ability to be flexible. I use the word "innate" because some experts believe that flexibility is an innate trait of a person. Through a combination of nature and nurture, we each have a different tendency to be flexible. My favorite test that reveals one's flexibility, among many other personality traits, is Emergenetics. Emergenetics is a test that was designed to determine your thinking and behavioral attributes, and to compare them to the general population. I've taken the Emergenetics test several times and each time it has shown that my tendency to be flexible is low. This could reveal itself as being stubborn in certain situations or it could also be seen as conviction and determination about my point of view. Either way, knowing that I have that strong tendency can help me develop techniques to improve my flexibility and help my partner understand my behavior when discussing contentious topics. I highly recommend you take the Emergenetics exam to understand your thinking and behavioral attributes more clearly. The website is https://www.emergenetics.com/take-a-profile/

If you or your partner want to explore compromise more, here are some resources.

My ability and willingness to compromise:

	Partner A	Partner B
I'm not interested in compromising		
It's possible but will be infrequent		
Yes, I'll compromise but it should be situational		
I am open to compromising on almost anything		
Definitely, I'll always compromise		
Other (explain)		

My receptivity to learning more about compromise and developing this skill:

	Partner A	Partner B
Zero		
Reluctant but convincible		
Open to spending a little time on this		
Open to it but let's discuss how much		
Fully committed, let's make it happen		
Other (explain)		

Rate your view of importance to success of a blended family:

	Partner A	Partner B
Rating (1=low, 10=high)		

Now that you've gone through the assessment, figure out a plan to address any gaps or differences that need to be explored further or require additional discussion.

Topics to Discuss

| |
| |
| |
| |
| |

Action Plans

Steps we will take to address the topics, issues, or challenges we identified in the section above.

| |
| |
| |
| |
| |

Online Resources

1) The 5 rules of fair compromise in a relationship http://www.bodyandsoul.com.au/sex-relationships/relationships/the-5-rules-of-fair-compromise-in-a-relationship/news-story/3829c1e92ca2d777ef33bb5af2d2925e

2) How Much Should You Compromise for Your Relationship? https://www.psychologytoday.com/blog/maybe-its-just-me/201106/how-much-should-you-compromise-your-relationship

3) When to Compromise in a Relationship (& When to Say No Way) https://www.meetmindful.com/when-to-compromise-in-a-relationship/

4) 7 Ways Learning To Compromise Improves All Your Relationships
   http://www.lifehack.org/articles/communication/7-ways-learning-compromise-
   improves-all-your-relationships.html

5) Good Compromise vs. Bad Compromise http://www.oprah.com/relationships/good-
   compromise-vs-bad-compromise

Books

1) On Relationships: Embracing Love in Delicious Complicity
   by Joseph Civitella

2) Mike & Margareth's No-Nonsense Guide for Couples: How to Manage Conflict,
   Communication & Compromise in Your Relationships by Michael Sands and Margareth
   Garnier

3) Marriage is all about Compromise -To Care and To Protect: Partners in Love are partners
   in Real Life by Subhash Chandra Thakur and Larry Thakur

4) Getting Past the Pain Between Us: Healing and Reconciliation Without Compromise
   (Nonviolent Communication Guides) by Marshall B. Rosenberg

SKILL 8 - ADAPTABILITY

Adaptability is defined as being to adjust to new circumstances. Wow, this is an important key because you are certain to be faced with numerous new circumstances throughout a blended family relationship. Just think about how much the kids, themselves, will change throughout their youth. Then factor in changes due to you and your partner aging, jobs, overall family, friends, economy and more. If you go into a new blended family without the capacity to learn and grow as the family and environment change, you're potentially going to be facing far more conflict than necessary. It's vital to embrace the mindset that each circumstance or phase in a blended family relationship represents a learning opportunity. Most of us just let new situations happen and then we chalk up that learning experience and hope for the best the next time. Being truly adaptable means that you consciously learn from each experience and are intentional about adjusting your response when that occurs again. The best way to make that experience really sink in is to educate yourself about it beyond your firsthand experience. With the volume of information now available via the internet, we all have massive amounts of research, opinions, and other types of resources to help us learn and grow.

A good example of where adaptability would come in is when the first time a step-child is defiant to the non-biological parent. For many people, this could be a non-issue if you're accepting of the fact that stepchildren and step-parents will inherently experience a little conflict. For those not understanding that dynamic, they might first feel outrage and attempt to use power or volume to overcome that resistance. Regardless of how you react initially, use your adaptability to educate yourself on the dynamics of the situation and what experts say about how to handle it. Once you deconstruct what's going on in the child's mind and learn a few tools and techniques to deal with it, you'll be much more equipped to deal with it next time it happens. Believe me, there will be plenty of opportunities to learn if you're a step-parent!

Story: Another story I picked up along the way described how adaptability is so important for both partners when joining a new blended family. In this case, a man moved in with his girlfriend and her three kids. He had partial custody of his child, so at certain times there would be four children and the couple in the home. It didn't take long to realize that his parenting style was much different than his girlfriend's. He immediately took the role of disciplinarian of his girlfriend's children because that's the role he had with his child. When he was confronted with how much this was negatively affecting his girlfriend's children and how much it was limiting their ability to develop a relationship with him, he resisted the notion that he was the one who should change. He wasn't willing to consider that he was the one moving into this home with rules already well-established and maybe it wasn't appropriate for him to exert his new rules without any conversation with his partner or her children. Had he embraced being more adaptable and open to understanding the circumstances, they all could have avoided several months of difficulty and an uncertain long-term future.

My capacity to be adaptable:

	Partner A	Partner B
No ability to adapt to changes		
I can adapt occasionally, depends on the situation		
I am willing and able to adapt most of the time		
Highly adaptable		
I'm a chameleon		
Other (explain)		

My receptivity to learning more about being more adaptable:

	Partner A	Partner B
Zero		
Reluctant but convincible		
Open to spending a little time on this		
Open to it but let's discuss how much		
Fully committed, let's make it happen		
Other (explain)		

Rate your view of importance to success of a blended family:

	Partner A	Partner B
Rating (1=low, 10=high)		

Now that you've gone through the assessment, create a plan to address any gaps or differences that need to be explored further or require additional discussion.

Topics to Discuss

Action Plans

Some steps we will take to address the topics, issues or challenges we identified in the section above.

Online Resources

1. Adaptability in Relationships http://herviewfromhome.com/adaptability-in-relationships/

2. Real Families, Real Answers: Adaptability http://realfamiliesrealanswers.org/?page_id=13

3. 10 Ways To Improve Your Adaptability https://www.keynoteresource.com/article3tonyallesandra.html

4. Everyone Wins with Adaptability – How Adaptable Are You? http://www.fripp.com/everyone-wins-with-adaptability-how-adaptable-are-you/

SKILL 9 - PICK YOUR BATTLES

I've already covered adaptability and compromise, but this topic warrants extra discussion. I think it's very important to realize that certain topics you'll face in your blended family relationship are going to be more personal and more important to you, and others will be more personal and important to your partner. Perhaps one of you had a childhood experience that made one topic like cleaning your room much more personal and sensitive. Maybe one of you crashed a car while out past curfew and now you're really sensitive and overly worried that it might happen to one of the children. Trust me that there will be many different topics you have to deal with in your relationship that vary in degree of importance to each partner. It is incumbent upon each of you to recognize that and not attempt to get your way or battle over every little issue that comes up. Seek to understand your partner's point of view and consider why something may be more important to him or her. If it's not something you really need to stand your ground on, then don't. You'll have plenty of other opportunities to hold firm on issues you have a stronger conviction about.

Another important point to share on this topic is you should step back once in a while and regain a perspective on what is important in life and what's not worth spending the emotional capital disputing. From my experience, it's easy to get sucked into fretting and battling over little disagreements in a new blended family. You feel like you lost a small battle about one issue so you're intent on winning the next one. Next thing you know, you've got a lengthy list of petty disputes about small, relatively meaningless things. Relationships can erode quickly when every aspect of your home life is a small battle ground. Regularly find time to appreciate what is positive about your partner, your home, and your blended family. Be thankful and show appreciation as much as possible, so you don't get dragged down into the abyss of little battles. It's ok to stand up for those issues you feel are most important, but pick those carefully in order to maintain a loving, happy household.

My final point is children typically don't react well when there are rules for every single behavior and action they have. In my experience, you can't govern their behavior, actions, homework, cleanliness, personal care, etc. 24x7. Excessive structure and oversight can be smothering and can cause them to react in an opposite way than a parent intends. Pick the battles you feel are most important in their growth and development. You, as parents, should provide boundaries, rules, consequences, etc., but they also need a little latitude to make mistakes and learn from them. Choose your battles carefully so you get their attention with the topics that mean the most and you don't dilute their attention and focus by fretting over every little thing. If you're a step-parent attempting to impart a rule or some wisdom on a step-child, you will particularly need to be sensitive to how much you exert your opinions and rules on them. Let's face it, step-parent - child relationships are complicated. There are MANY resources available to explore that, so I won't go deep down that path now.

My capacity to be selective about issues I pursue:

	Partner A	**Partner B**
I'll say what's on my mind every time		
I am willing to consider being more selective about issues I raise		
I am committed to working on this		
I'm usually very sensitive to this and will continue to work on it		
No problem at all, I'm already very cautious about which topics I choose to discuss		
Other (explain)		

My receptivity to learning to be more selective about which battles I choose to pick:

	Partner A	Partner B
Zero		
Reluctant but convincible		
Open to spending a little time on this		
Open to it but let's discuss how much		
Fully committed, let's make it happen		
Other (explain)		

Rate your view of importance to success of a blended family:

	Partner A	Partner B
Rating (1=low, 10=high)		

Now that you've gone through the assessment, figure out a plan to address any gaps or differences that need to be explored further or require additional discussion.

Topics to Discuss

Action Plans

Steps we will take to address the topics, issues or challenges we identified in the section above.

Online Resources

1) How to Pick Your Battles http://www.parenting.com/article/how-to-pick-your-battles
2) Expert Tips for Picking Your Relationship Battles Wisely http://abcnews.go.com/Lifestyle/expert-tips-picking-relationship-battles-wisely/story?id=30116974
3) Choose Your Battles: Fighting Less in Relationships http://tinybuddha.com/blog/choose-your-battles-fighting-less-in-relationships/
4) How to Choose Your Battles and Fight for What Actually Matters http://lifehacker.com/5989295/how-to-choose-your-battles-and-fight-for-what-actually-matters

5) How to Most Effectively Pick Your Battles

   http://www.sixwise.com/newsletters/05/05/25/how-to-most-effectively-pick-your-battles.htm

Books

1) PICK and CHOOSE YOUR BATTLES by CHERYL COLLINSON

2) Ending the Parent-Teen Control Battle: Resolve the Power Struggle and Build Trust, Responsibility, and Respect

   by Neil D. Brown and Donald T Saposnek

3) Discipline Children: How To Stop The Battles And Develop A Healthy Relationship With Your Child by Ariel Stefan

4) Calmer, Easier, Happier Parenting: Five Strategies That End the Daily Battles and Get Kids to Listen the First by Noel Janis-Norton

5) Achieving Success with Impossible Children: How to win the battle of Wills by Dave Ziegler

SKILL 10 - YOU TELL ME

I'd love to hear more thoughts on keys you've found essential to your success. Please email me at mat@blendbutdontbreak.com and share your stories.

SKILL 10 - YOU TELL ME

CHAPTER 4: ASSESSING PHILOSOPHICAL ALIGNMENT

A long-held truth is one of mine
Many beacons in my life that shine

Principles as fixed as rock
Each paradigm a building block

Are they deep in how they're set
Such that adjusting is a long bet

Compromise is how we align
Without some give we won't be fine

The purpose of this section is to facilitate discussion between you and your partner to help you identify each other's philosophy on common blended family topics. If you're contemplating blending a family, this will help you understand if there are big philosophic gaps before you commit to moving in together. If you already are in a blended family, this will help you clarify your position on key philosophical gaps so you can focus your efforts to resolve them more effectively.

As you go through this, you may find you're developing a long list of topics that you don't completely agree on. This is natural whether you're going into a blended family or any new relationship. By identifying the topics and discussing them ahead of time, you're putting yourself way ahead of many other couples who just bang into these issues after they're already living together. Once you're living together, the tension and pressure surrounding a topic can be much more significant and can interfere with finding a simple peaceful resolution. If you can discuss these topics prior to moving in together, you can address tough issues with no stress or pressure to fix something at the moment. The ancillary emotions that complicate resolution won't exist, so both partners can keep positive, constructive mindsets as they discuss.

Here are a few proposed *rules of engagement* before you begin discussing these topics.

1. Spend time alone thinking about each topic and clarifying your thoughts before discussing them with your partner.

2. Don't attempt to solve everything in one sitting. It will be impossible. Spread out your discussions over a period of time, possibly weeks or months.

3. Prioritize your list so you don't attempt to discuss the most difficult topics in one sitting.

4. Set aside 30-60 min initially and make sure you have a quiet, stress-free environment.

5. Use soft music or lighting to help set a mood of comfort and acceptance. Personally, I like to listen to "chill" music when relaxing. It's easy to find chill stations on the mainstream music streaming services.

6. Find a comfortable, quiet setting and put all electronics or other distractions away. Face your partner when in discussion so you're both concentrating and engaged.

7. Celebrate quick wins when you find you're both in agreement on various topics. Show each other love and affection and keep it fun.

8. Don't argue. Don't argue. Don't argue. If you find that a topic turns into an argument, drop it and come back to it later in that day or another day. Don't freakin' argue.

9. If you reach a sticky topic, write down your thoughts so you both have a clear position on it. Also write down where you would be willing to compromise.

10. Compromise is key, so choose to concede in a few areas so your partner will do the same in others.

11. Approach all discussions with the mindset of love. If your partner has a differing opinion on something that you wildly disagree with, respect that opinion and seek to understand him/her. Your love for that person should compel you to want to understand rather than judge.

12. Avoid discussing these topics when alcohol is involved. It can cause people to overreact and create conflict. It might be a nice tension-reliever, but be aware of the risks.

13. Do some research on how others approach these topics. Reach out to friends to get insight or advice. Also, browse the web for articles and websites. There's a vast amount of information about all of the topics listed in the discussion guide section.

14. Use a professional for the issues you can't resolve. There might be very emotional, contentious issues that you just can't seem to resolve. Get the help of a counselor to help you talk through difficult topics. Also consider either a mediator or lawyer to provide guidance where there are legal issues involved.

Now it's time to begin the alignment process. The first topic is going to be a challenging one, but will likely be one of the top issues any blended family with children involved will face. Remember, load up your empathy, love and flexibility and you'll do fine.

PARENTING STYLE

Parenting style is defined as "a psychological construct representing standard strategies that parents use in their child rearing." Regardless of whether you're bringing in children from a prior relationship or plan to have children as a new blended family, it's vital to establish common ground on parenting styles. This has the potential to be the most contentious topic in your new blended family, so a proper investment in clarifying your own thoughts and feelings on the topic and discussing it thoroughly with your partner will prove to be very useful.

If you're planning to join a blended family where your partner has children and you don't, this is probably a topic you haven't thought about much. Before you move in and get under the pressure of many new situations, it's a great idea to think about your philosophy and beliefs regarding parenting style. There are many notable experts that have written on the topic of how our approach to parenting was imprinted on us by our parents and our experiences at each stage of our development as children. Therefore, even if you haven't raised children before, you can reflect on your experiences and use that as a guide for how you think you would address various situations that will come up.

It's important to point out there are very different parent-child interactions between parent and biological child(ren) and parent and non-biological child(ren.) My first-hand experience has been that it is easy to get defensive and protective of your biological child when your partner is trying to create or reinforce a rule, punishment, etc. Your instinctual reaction as the biological parent is to protect your child, when the situation might perfectly warrant the interaction from your partner and child. It's very important to understand that sensitivities could exist in the simplest of interactions. If you are aware of this dynamic, you both can potentially approach situations with the children differently so you avoid unnecessary conflict.

If you need guidance on how to define your parenting style, you can either do online research or just read through this simple model to see where you fit.

1) **Authoritative:** Authoritative parenting is characterized by a child-centered approach that holds high expectations of maturity. Authoritative parents can understand how their children are feeling and teach them how to regulate their feelings.

2) **Authoritarian:** Authoritarian parenting is a restrictive, punishment-heavy parenting style in which parents make their children follow their directions with little to no explanation or feedback and focus on the child's and family's perception and status.

3) **Indulgent/ Permissive:** Indulgent parenting is a style of parenting in which parents are very involved with their children but place few demands or controls on them." Parents are nurturing and accepting, and are responsive to the child's needs and wishes.

4) **Neglectful:** This is a style characterized by a lack of responsiveness to a child's needs. Uninvolved parents make few to no demands of their children and they are often indifferent, dismissive or even completely neglectful.

I recommend reviewing wikipedia to start with if you don't identify with one of these four styles. Wiki lists several other styles as follows: positive, concerted cultivation, narcissistic, nurturant, overparenting, slow, idle, dolphin and more.

Instructions

The objective is for you and your partner to check the box that best fits your philosophy on each topic. This will help you each clarify your own position on the topic, allow you both to understand how aligned you are, and give you a better basis from which to discuss the topic. This will allow you to define some terms or create some compromises so parenting philosophy doesn't manifest as an issue while you're in your blended family.

My style for accountability/ rewards/ punishment for the children is:

	Partner A	Partner B
Rules must be strict and punishment is key to enforcement		
Spanking or physical reinforcement		
Clear rules, clear accountability with punishment		
Clear rules and guidelines with consequences like revoking privileges		
Define rules, but positive reinforcement only		
I decide how to punish mine, you decide how to punish yours		
Let them learn as they go		
Other		

Rate the level of importance for this topic:

	Partner A	Partner B
1 = low, 10 = high		

Discuss the differences in your choices for this topic and identify a few issues or areas that need resolution or compromise.

My preferences for curfews is:

	Partner A	**Partner B**
Strict curfew, no exceptions		
Curfew depends on the child's age, consequences for being late		
Curfew is negotiable, depends on circumstances		
Set a curfew, allow for flexibility		
Keep it loose as long as they check in periodically		
Let the children come home when they want		
Other		

Rate the level of importance for this topic:

	Partner A	Partner B
1 = low, 10 = high		

Discuss the differences in your choices for this topic and identify some areas or issues that need resolution or compromise.

My preferences for the children's bedtime:

	Partner A	Partner B
Strict guidelines, punishment if they don't adhere		
Set guidelines, but use best effort to stick to it		
Set rules depending on age, not too strict		
Be flexible, depends on the night		
They can go to bed when they choose		
Other (explain)		

Rate the level of importance for this topic:

	Partner A	Partner B
1 = low, 10 = high		

Discuss the differences in your choices for this topic and identify a few areas or issues that need resolution or compromise.

My philosophy for use of electronics (phones, games, computers):

	Partner A	Partner B
Strict policies, adherence and parental controls on everything		
Moderate guidelines and monitoring		
Set guidelines, use best effort to reinforce, some monitoring		
Set guidelines if it becomes an issue		
No limits on duration of use or time of day		
Other (explain)		

My view of children dating is:

	Partner A	Partner B
No dating allowed until they are 18		
Strict guidelines, significant oversight		
Clear guidelines, trust but verify		
Set guidelines but give them plenty of leeway		
They set their own rules		
Other		

Rate the level of importance for this topic:

	Partner A	Partner B
1 = low, 10 = high		

Discuss the differences in your choices for this topic and identify a few aspects that need resolution or compromise.

My preferences for TV viewing for the children:

	Partner A	Partner B
Strict oversight of time allowed and content		
Clear rules, monitoring is best effort		
Guidelines depend on age, leeway on content		
Loose guidelines on amount and content		
They can watch whatever they want		
Other (explain)		

Rate the level of importance for this topic:

	Partner A	Partner B
1 = low, 10 = high		

Discuss the differences in your choices for this topic and identify a few aspects that need resolution or compromise.

My expectations for the children with homework and school performance is:

	Partner A	Partner B
High expectations for completing homework, attendance and grades		
Set expectations and monitor closely. High involvement but no pressure		
Involved in homework and conferences but best effort is fine		
Answer questions and be supportive but not highly involved in homework or conferences		
Get them where they need to be but results are up to them		
Kids should be self-sufficient, not going to be too involved		
Other		

Rate the level of importance for this topic:

	Partner A	Partner B
1 = low, 10 = high		

Discuss the differences in your choices for this topic and identify some areas or issues that need resolution or compromise.

My philosophy for how children should interact with parents:

	Partner A	Partner B
Be seen but not heard. Kids should play and entertain themselves		
Parents are involved but only for basic care and needs		
Spend as much time as a family as we can but parents need alone time too		
Find a balance between tending to the kids' needs and fostering the couple's relationship		
It's a parent's role to be devoted to care, deep interaction and involvement throughout the day		
Other		

Rate the level of importance for this topic:

	Partner A	Partner B
1 = low, 10 = high		

Discuss the differences in your choices for this topic and identify a few issues that need resolution or compromise.

My view on parental respect by the children is:

	Partner A	Partner B
Respect at all times is a must. Consequences are a must when it's not shown		
Respect is an important value and parents must regularly reinforce it		
Respect is just one of many values that should be gently reinforced		
Help the children learn respect through positive reinforcement and love		
It's not a huge concern, let it evolve as it may		
Other		

Rate the level of importance for this topic:

	Partner A	Partner B
1 = low, 10 = high		

Discuss the differences in your choices for this topic and identify some areas or issues that need resolution or compromise.

My own important topic is _____

	Partner A	Partner B

Rate the level of importance for this topic:

	Partner A	Partner B
1 = low, 10 = high		

Discuss the differences in your choices for this topic and identify a few areas or issues that need resolution or compromise.

Certainly, the topics above don't encompass every important issue related to parenting style. Below are more potential topics. If none of these capture your most important issues, then make your own list and follow the process to examine the similarities and differences between you and your partner

Topics To Discuss:
- ❏ Reward or punishment
- ❏ Consequences
- ❏ Communication style with the children
- ❏ Daily schedules/ routines
- ❏ Dating parameters for teens
- ❏ Work/ earning income expectations
- ❏ Safety
- ❏ Values
- ❏ Health and hygiene
- ❏ Exercise expectations
- ❏ Hobbies
- ❏ Worship/ religious practices

FINANCES

It almost goes without saying that money and finances are often one of the most contentious issues in any relationship. It is noted widely as one of the biggest causes of divorce in the US. When you add in more complexity with blended family issues, it becomes clear that discussing this topic with your partner thoroughly before you blend your family can help avoid conflict and difficulty. You should think of this topic in terms of what each of you are bringing into the partnership, how to budget and spend what you earn during your partnership, and what you want to do with money long-term for yourselves, the children, and, potentially, extended family members.

This is a whopper of a topic and not everyone is equipped with the right background to effectively discuss all these topics or come up with a solution for how to handle every issue. Proactively engage a financial planner, investment counselor, estate attorney, or related expert if you need guidance.

My overall financial philosophy is:

	Partner A	Partner B
Captain frugal, set the bar		
Penny pincher, clipping coupons		
Conservative		
Budgeter but spender		
Spontaneous, loose spender		
Make it rain, plenty to go around		
Other (describe)		

Rate the level of importance for this topic:

	Partner A	Partner B
1 = low, 10 = high		

Discuss the differences in your choices for this topic and identify some areas or issues that need resolution or compromise.

My preference for how finances are managed is:

	Partner A	Partner B
I control the finances		
Strict, but I'm willing to compromise on a few things		
50/50 decision-making		
Clear rules, one person manages finances but flexible		
Loose budget, decide as we go		
We share decisions, don't need too much structure		
Other (explain)		

Rate the level of importance for this topic:

	Partner A	Partner B
1 = low, 10 = high		

Discuss the differences in your choices for this topic and identify some areas or issues that need resolution or compromise.

My preference for banking is:

	Partner A	Partner B
Separate accounts for everything		
Shared bank account but separate retirement accounts		
Shared accounts for everything		
Shared accounts but clear rules around spending limits/ budget		
Let's figure it out as we go		
Other		

Rate the level of importance for this topic:

	Partner A	Partner B
1 = low, 10 = high		

Discuss the differences in your choices for this topic and identify any areas or issues that need resolution or compromise.

How we plan to handle money or assets we bring into the blended family:

	Partner A	Partner B
I keep everything I previously had separate		
We need a prenuptial agreement		
We can share but let's negotiate some things		
Equal split, but let's put it in writing		
Mine is yours, yours is mine		
Other (explain)		

Rate the level of importance for this topic:

	Partner A	Partner B
1 = low, 10 = high		

Discuss the differences in your choices for this topic and identify a few aspects that need resolution or compromise.

How we plan to pay for housing purchase or rental and ongoing costs:

	Partner A	**Partner B**
I'll pay for initial housing and ongoing costs		
All costs should be split proportional to income		
All costs should be split 50/50		
It should be in the budget and solved with every other expense		
Let's just figure it out as we go		
Other (explain)		

Rate the level of importance for this topic:

	Partner A	Partner B
1 = low, 10 = high		

Discuss the differences in your choices for this topic and identify some aspects that need resolution or compromise.

Our plan to finance our education or our children's education:

	Partner A	Partner B
I pay for my education or my kid's education, you pay for yours		
The ex is responsible for the kid's education, not me or us		
We budget together and share all costs		
My kids are our kids, just another shared expense		
Let's make a rough plan and adjust as needed		
Figure it out as we go		
Other		

Rate the level of importance for this topic:

	Partner A	Partner B
1 = low, 10 = high		

Discuss the differences in your choices for this topic and identify a few aspects that need resolution or compromise.

How we will handle expenses for the children (activities/ sports, healthcare, clothing, dental/ orthodontics, primary education expenses, etc.):

	Partner A	Partner B
I pay for mine, you pay for yours		
Let's make a list and decide what to split		
Split expenses according to income		
Split costs but stick to a budget		
The ex should pay for everything		
Shared expenses, like everything else		
Other		

Rate the level of importance for this topic:

	Partner A	Partner B
1 = low, 10 = high		

Discuss the differences in your choices for this topic and identify some aspects that need resolution or compromise.

My preferences for retirement planning are:

	Partner A	Partner B
Save the max amount		
Follow a financial planner's advice		
Mutually decide on what to put away		
Tuck money away as opportunity arises		
YOLO, who needs retirement		
Other (explain)		

Rate the level of importance for this topic:

	Partner A	Partner B
1 = low, 10 = high		

Discuss the differences in your choices for this topic and identify a few aspects that need resolution or compromise.

Other Potential Topics To Discuss:

❏ Joint or shared bank accounts

❏ Financial contribution to a new home or rental

❏ Proceeds from sale of former homes

❏ Division of rental income

❏ Maintenance costs on a shared home/ rental

❏ Upgrades and enhancements to a shared home/ rental

❏ Cost of utilities

❏ Day-to-day expenses for kids (healthcare, extracurricular activities, school supplies, clothes, etc.)

❏ How to handle child support or spousal support

❏ Household budgeting

❏ Retirement planning

❏ Division of inherited money, property or assets

❏ Vacations

❏ Week-to-week entertainment

❏ Primary or secondary education expenses for the adults and children

❏ Payment of pre-existing student loans

❏ Care for aging/ elderly parents

❏ Keep going if you have other topics to discuss

HOUSE RULES

You might think that organically coming up with some basic rules for how to operate your home would be easy. I can tell you from first-hand experience that when you try to do this while already living together, the difficulty can increase exponentially. If one partner or the other has very strong feelings about certain house rules, that agitation can make negotiating very challenging. It's so much easier to lay down your proverbial house rule cards before you move in so you can find out how close or far apart you are on core issues. Since you should have already discussed parenting styles in a previous section, that should enable you to stick to the specifics of the rules you want to have and not get caught up in how you choose to reinforce them.

My preference for main living area cleanliness is:

	Partner A	Partner B
Immaculate		
Almost always tidy		
Clean but not obsessed		
A little messy		
Clean only when necessary		
Living with the pigs		
Other (explain)		

Rate the level of importance for this topic:

	Partner A	Partner B
1 = low, 10 = high		

Discuss the differences in your choices for this topic and identify a few aspects that need resolution or compromise.

My preference for cleanliness of the child(ren)'s room is:

	Partner A	Partner B
Always immaculate		
Tidy 3-4x per week		
Beds made, tidy 1-2x per week		
Tidy 1x per week		
Let it be what it may		
Other (explain)		

Rate the level of importance for this topic:

	Partner A	Partner B
1 = low, 10 = high		

Discuss the differences in your choices for this topic and identify some aspects that need resolution or compromise.

My preference for condition of the yard, lawn, landscaping is:

	Partner A	Partner B
Someone tends to it every day		
Mow, trim, weed 2-3x per week		
Mow, trim, weed 1x per week		
Address it as needed, not a big concern		
Outsource it, we don't touch it		
Other (explain)		

Rate the level of importance for this topic:

	Partner A	Partner B
1 = low, 10 = high		

Discuss the differences in your choices for this topic and identify a few aspects that need resolution or compromise.

My style for dealing with the kitchen during or after meals is:

	Partner A	Partner B
Kitchen must be spotless after every meal		
I cook, you clean up		
I cook, the kids clean up		
We cook, figure out the mess later		
I'm a chef, my mess is my creativity		
Other (explain)		

Rate the level of importance for this topic:

	Partner A	Partner B
1 = low, 10 = high		

Discuss the differences in your choices for this topic and identify some aspects that need resolution or compromise.

My preference for assigning chores to the children is:

	Partner A	Partner B
Strict chores, strict consequences		
Well-defined chores, positive reinforcement to follow		
General guidelines and loose consequences		
Define chores as needed		
Outsource it, who cares		
Other (explain)		

Rate the level of importance for this topic:

	Partner A	Partner B
1 = low, 10 = high		

Discuss the differences in your choices for this topic and identify a few aspects that need resolution or compromise.

My preference for spring or fall clean-up is:

	Partner A	Partner B
Total purge 2x per year, we all work		
Thorough cleaning, kids involved as needed		
Deal with specific areas, nothing big		
We hoard and we're proud		
Other (explain)		

Rate the level of importance for this topic:

	Partner A	Partner B
1 = low, 10 = high		

Discuss the differences in your choices for this topic and identify some aspects that need resolution or compromise.

My preference for dealing with laundry is:

	Partner A	Partner B
Everyone does their own		
I wash, everyone folds and puts away		
Adults do it as needed, loose rules		
Responsibility rotates between adults and kids		
Other (explain)		

Rate the level of importance for this topic:

	Partner A	Partner B
1 = low, 10 = high		

Discuss the differences in your choices for this topic and identify a few aspects that need resolution or compromise.

How pet feeding, grooming and cleaning is handled:

	Partner A	Partner B
Adults handle it all		
Kids are assigned various responsibilities, strict adherence		
Kids are assigned various responsibilities, positive reinforcement		
We all just do whatever is necessary, no big deal		
Someone just take care of it when it gets really bad		
Other (explain)		

Deal-breakers I have when it comes to house rules are:

Partner A
Partner B

Pool and/or hot tub responsibilities are:

	Partner A	Partner B
I handle it all		
Adults alternate duties on tight schedule		
Adults alternate duties as needed		
Children have duties, tight schedule		
Children have duties, involved as needed		
Outsource it, who cares		
Other (explain)		

Rate the level of importance for this topic:

	Partner A	Partner B
1 = low, 10 = high		

Discuss the differences in your choices for this topic and identify some aspects of the topic that need resolution or compromise.

Topics To Discuss:

- ❑ Cleanliness philosophies of each partner (neat-freak, orderly, messy, horder)
- ❑ Setting expectations with children and following up
- ❑ Communicating rules
- ❑ Consequences when rules aren't followed
- ❑ Deal-breaker rules vs nice-to-have
- ❑ Household chores for adults and children (what and how often)
  - ❑ Bedrooms
  - ❑ Clothes/ laundry
  - ❑ Kitchen
  - ❑ Common areas
  - ❑ Garage
  - ❑ Spring/ Fall cleanup
- ❑ Pet feeding, grooming and cleanup
- ❑ Outdoor chores for adults and children

❑ Lawn/ yard
❑ Landscaping
❑ Windows
❑ Bushes/ shrubs/ trees
❑ Weeds
❑ Animals

STEP PARENTING

Whether one or both partners are bringing children into the blended family, there will be at least one stepparent. If neither partner has ever been a stepparent or grown up around one, this will be a very important area to focus on. Being a stepparent might be one of life's greatest challenges. It is easy to view being a stepparent as much more difficult than being a "typical" parent. I'm going to reference an article from 2015 from the website stepmomhelp.com that identifies the **top seven reasons** why step parenting is more difficult than parenting.

1. Children are more forgiving of a parent than a stepparent.
2. A parent has a higher level of tolerance for their own child than the stepparent has.
3. A stepparent never knows when they should speak up.
4. The child wants to be parented by their parent, not their stepparent.
5. Children naturally want to please their parents, not so with stepparents.
6. A parent has unconditional love for their child, whereas a stepchild can feel like a foreign entity to a stepparent.
7. There might be an unhappy ex in the mix, discouraging the kids from having a relationship with the stepparent.

If you'd like to read more of the reasoning behind each point, you can access the original article at http://www.stepmomhelp.com/why-stepparenting-is-harder-than-parenting/.

The purpose of this guide is to facilitate discussion and not provide all the answers to the complexities of stepparenting. Rest assured, though, there are abundant resources for educating yourself on this topic. A healthy dose of reading and research in addition to aligning expectations with your partner will be a great enabler of future success.

The step-parent's role in paying for the children's expenses (regardless of biological or non-biological) is:

	Partner A	Partner B
Biological parent pays for all biological child(ren) expenses		
The split of expenses for non-biological child(ren) is negotiable		
Once married, all household and children expenses are shared expenses		
The highest earner will pay for child(ren) expenses		
It's not a concern, we will figure it out as we go		
Other (explain)		

Rate the level of importance for this topic:

	Partner A	Partner B
1 = low, 10 = high		

Discuss the differences in your choices for this topic and identify a few aspects that need resolution or compromise.

The role of the step-parent in enforcing rules and discipline for the child(ren) is:

	Partner A	Partner B
The step-parent should have full authority to enforce rules and discipline the child(ren)		
Both parents should enforce rules but only the biological parent should discipline the child(ren)		
Only the biological parent should enforce rules and discipline		
Not sure, let's agree on the approach together		
Let's not have too many rules, keep it loose		
There's no room for discipline of any sort.		
Other (explain)		

Rate the level of importance for this topic:

	Partner A	Partner B
1 = low, 10 = high		

Discuss the differences in your choices for this topic and identify some aspects that need resolution or compromise.

My belief about how much each parent should be involved with raising the child(ren):

	Partner A	Partner B
It's the biological parent's role to raise the child(ren), not the step-parent		
The step-parent should have at least a little involvement		
Both parents should have equal involvement regardless of biological connection		
Whomever is the better parent should take the lead and do more of the parenting		
I prefer a nanny or family member do most of the caretaking, parents have a limited role		
Other (explain)		

Rate the level of importance for this topic:

	Partner A	Partner B
1 = low, 10 = high		

Discuss the differences in your choices for this topic and identify some aspects that need resolution or compromise.

Partner A's concerns about step-parenting:

Partner B's concerns about step-parenting:

Things we can do to ensure that we have a healthy step-parenting experience in our blended family:

A few ways the step-parent can develop a bond and relationship with the non-biological child(ren):

INTEGRATING THE CHILDREN

Children typically have an amazing ability to adjust to changes in the family when divorce occurs or a new blended family is built, but you can't totally take for granted that every child will easily adjust to major changes in housing, parental relationships, school changes, etc. I personally had to adapt to changes due to three divorces in my family while growing up. I moved homes three times and changed schools twice. I had step-siblings visit for prolonged periods of time that displaced me from my room. I experienced my father moving at least five times and he never lived in the same state as I did. As a result, I was only able to see my Dad once or twice a year for a long weekend or a week's vacation. I had a step-mother come in and out of my life as well as several of Dad's serious girlfriends. I also experienced several of my Mom's boyfriends come in and out of our lives until she gave up on dating and settled with mostly being alone. As I look back on it, this amounted to a great deal of adversity, change, and periodic turmoil. However, I think I rolled with the changes pretty well. I didn't really know any better, so I didn't develop an attitude because all this change was happening to me. I just did my best to roll with the changes and not let it affect me too much. Don't get me wrong, I can recall plenty of difficult circumstances all this change caused. There are some bad memories and emotional scars, butI always look back on it as the stepping stones to where I am now. I look at the experiences to find motivation and drive. I look at the pain and find courage and empathy for my kids.

I have also always been amazed at how my children have overcome the adversity and difficulty of divorce. They've had to adjust to life with a new step-father. They've moved with me twice and survived the unsuccessful blended family attempt. For the majority of their childhood, they've had to move back and forth between two households every week. Especially as teens, this was not an easy task for them to keep track of their favorite possessions and transport them each time they swapped between my house and their mom's. There's no question that this experience was challenging, but they've done an amazing job of adapting to the changes. I'm very grateful that they have continued to perform well in school, stay very active with sports and other activities, and have friendships.

Just because my kids and I managed to get through these experiences intact doesn't mean all the children of blended families do. New blended family parents should be concerned with the emotional impact this could have on the children. I can confidently say that every child heading into a new blended family will have questions, concerns and anxiety. However, the more you involve your children in the process, the more likely you are to quickly transition to a new, happy family.

There are many aspects of change the children could face and you have to pick and choose which topics are appropriate to include them in. I highly recommend that you involve them in whatever discussions are appropriate for the age of the kids. The more they feel included, the more they will buy into the new family, new home, and new rules. It will be very difficult to find peace and happiness in a new blended family if one or more of the children are strongly dissenting.

I encourage you to consider the guidance of a professional as you consider how to involve children in the planning of a new blended family. It is certainly not required, but the structure and experience of a professional can offer an environment that is safe and moderated so emotions and feelings can be expressed freely. A professional can also be a neutral third party that the children can speak freely with and vent to without fear of reaction from a parent. A professional can also detect warning signs and other potential triggers that a child has developed from the damage of a difficult divorce. If the parents can be aware of the biggest sensitivities of the children, they can plan ahead and be careful to deal with those more carefully.

My relationship with the child(ren) is:

	Partner A	Partner B
Too new to rate it		
Very strained or damaged		
Amicable but not close		
Not close, not strained		
Positive but room to grow		
Very healthy and loving		
Other (explain)		

Ideas to develop and strengthen the relationship with the children of the future blended family:

Concerns you have about the child(ren) as you plan your blended family:

Things we can do to help integrate the child(ren) into the blended family home:

Story: When I was about eight years old, I lived with my mother full-time and visited my father about once per year. At that time, my mother was remarried and my step-father had three kids from a prior marriage that were in the same age range as my sister and me. What made this version of our blended family particularly difficult was my step-father's kids would visit us a few times a year. There was usually a several week-long visit each summer. I recall it feeling somewhat like an invasion of our house that these three kids were there and my step-father would give them much more attention. This created feelings of jealousy and lead to conflict between my sister, me and our step-brothers and sister. Not knowing any better, we turned these feelings of confusion and jealousy into anger and aggression at our step-siblings. We argued over insignificant things and acted territorial instead of welcoming and friendly. I saw that verbal arguments were eventually replaced with pushing, shoving and hitting on occasion. My older sister became more protective of me and consequently more aggressive with them. I eventually came to dread those visits and saw those step-siblings as one big source of negativity in our lives.

Topics To Discuss:
- ❑ When to introduce the children to the new partner
- ❑ Activities or opportunities to enable the new partner to get to know the child(ren)
- ❑ Approach to informing the children about moving in together or a new engagement
- ❑ Ways to involve the children in choosing a new residence so they feel included
- ❑ Plan to involve the children (if age appropriate) in discussion about house rules, parenting styles, expectations
- ❑ Bedroom assignments; shared rooms or separate?
- ❑ Sharing of each child's toys or playthings
- ❑ Plans to continue an ongoing dialogue with the kids to allow them to provide feedback and share feelings and thoughts while the blended family is still new

Story: Terri used to travel for work and would often be gone for two to three days at a time. When she was gone, she would leave her kids, ages 5, 8, 10, at home with Tony, her second husband. As you might imagine, after getting home from a long trip, Terri was excited to see the kids and Tony. The kids were excited to see their mom and everyone wanted Terri's time and attention. For the first six months, Terri did her best to tend to her young children's needs and make sure they received enough attention and support after she was away. The kids had a decent relationship with Tony, but it's not the same as the closeness they had with mom. After about six months, Tony's frustration with her being gone and his disappointment that he wasn't the center of attention when she returned started to manifest itself. Tony started to resent the children and was angry when they demanded their mom's attention. Initially he joked about it a little bit and then started to make derisive comments directly to them. Occasionally, after a long, tiring trip, Terri would put the kids to bed and fall asleep in one of the kid's bed. This absolutely drove Tony crazy. On many occasions when this happened, he would lock the bedroom door and not let Terri back in until morning. On occasion, he would also leave the house and stay away for several hours because he knew that would make Terri feel bad. How could everyone wanting to show Terri some love when she returned from a trip turn into getting locked out of your bedroom for putting your kids to bed and falling asleep? In this case, Terri and Tony had poor communication skills and very different philosophical views on how much attention the children should receive. This was just one of many unsolvable challenges Terri and Tony had. They eventually were divorced after eight years of a mostly unhappy marriage.

Visits to Your Home

You might initially wonder why this is an important topic. When I was married about fifteen years ago, my wife and I invited my father and step-mother to live in my family's house for a few months to help during their transition from Michigan to Colorado. That couple of months turned into a year and my family had a few serious challenging experiences dealing with their prolonged stay. I predict most visits to a new blended family home won't last that long, but it certainly can become a very contentious topic if the couple isn't prepared.

On average, most of the visits you and your partner will have to contemplate are short visits by friends and family members. You will have in-laws visit over the holidays, friends stop in for a weekend, college pals come for a week or any number of scenarios that will cause your family both happiness and a little inconvenience and expense. It's helpful to talk through these logistics ahead of time so it doesn't become contentious just prior to the event.

Topics To Discuss:

- ❏ Frequency and duration of an in-law visit that both partners are comfortable with
- ❏ Frequency and duration of a family friend visit that both partners are comfortable with
- ❏ The room(s) that will be used to host visitors
- ❏ Arrangements the child(ren) need to make to accommodate visitors
- ❏ Advance notice both partners prefer prior to a family or friend visitor
- ❏ Willingness of each partner to allow a family member or friend to stay long-term
- ❏ Responsibility for preparing the room and cleaning up after visitors
- ❏ Arrangement on costs associated with hosting guests
- ❏ Openness each partner has to using a bedroom for a short-term rental (if applicable)

Legal

In the United States, there are different laws for every state that define the legalities and rights of couples co-habitating in an informal or legally recognized manner. A formal marriage is the most obvious official form of relationship. Common law marriage is another common form of relationship, but it does have gray areas. If you and your partner are getting married prior to blending your families and sharing a residence, then the best advice I can give is familiarize yourself with your state's laws in case there are any disputes about one or both partner's estates, property, assets, etc.

If you plan to have a blended family where there is not an imminent marriage planned, then you have more work to do to avoid potential discourse and disagreement. You may have already talked about a few financial topics in the Finances section, so this section is meant to clarify the extent legal documentation or guidance is necessary to make your arrangements official. I want to stress that you should engage legal professionals if you need guidance on any of these topics. You and your partner can talk about a few of these and create a common understanding, but many things won't withstand a future dispute unless they are in writing. I recommend that, at the very least, you and your partner should write down your arrangements and each retain a copy. While this won't be as foolproof as an agreement drafted by a lawyer, it will certainly be better than a verbal agreement.

Topics To Discuss:

- ❑ Are there assets such as property, cash, stocks, bonds, vehicles, campers/RVs, life insurance policies that require some documented agreement?
- ❑ Have both partners disclosed all debts and obligations and agreed on how they will be handled?
- ❑ Manner a family business income, debt and assets will be handled
- ❑ Plans to create or update a will, estate plan and/or living trust
- ❑ Agreement on living will, do not resuscitate order, organ donorship, and other matters related to severe health crises and death
- ❑ Is a prenuptial agreement required to protect pre-existing assets? For reference, here are items commonly included in a prenuptial agreement:
- ❑ Separate business
- ❑ Retirement benefits
- ❑ Income, deductions, and claims for filing your tax returns
- ❑ Management of household bills and expenses
- ❑ Management of joint bank accounts, if any
- ❑ Arrangement regarding investing in certain purchases or projects, like a house or business
- ❑ Management of credit card spending and payments
- ❑ Savings contributions
- ❑ Property distribution to the survivor, including life insurance, in the event of death
- ❑ Arranging putting one or the other through school
- ❑ Settlement of potential disagreements, such as using mediation or arbitration

Ex-spouses

Several of my friends have expressed that the biggest issue in their blended family is the drama and controversy caused by an ex-spouse. This can come in the form of being difficult to negotiate the children's schedule due to the inevitable changes required with school, activities, sports, etc. It can be related to financial matters such as child support, maintenance/ alimony, ad hoc children's expenses, future children's expenses and more. Factors such as jealousy of an ex-spouse or unpleasant interactions when both exes are at an event for the children can add stress. Perhaps an ex has just shirked his/her duties and it's a source of contention that the other parent and new parent have to pick up the slack. There are going to be many opportunities to interact with an ex-spouse when the children are growing up, and there is the potential for conflict all along the way.

Topics To Discuss:

- ❑ Concerns with amount of parenting time (too much or too little)
- ❑ Challenges with negotiating date changes for parenting time
- ❑ Pick up, drop off, or meet in between challenges
- ❑ Unfair share of child(ren)-related expenses
- ❑ Treatment of the child(ren) in the ex-spouse's home
- ❑ Ex-spouse talking negatively about a parent or stepparent
- ❑ Challenges with siblings at the ex-spouse's home
- ❑ Support for school work at the ex-spouse's home
- ❑ Other:_____

CHAPTER 5: THE KIDS ARE GROWN, IS THE BLEND OVER?!

Orange slices, apples, halftime snacks
Trophies, medals, pics and plaques

Concerts, plays, clubs and games
Encores, awards, recognition and fame

Geometry, history, literacy and biology
Calculus, physics, chemistry and physiology

Boyfriends, girlfriends, love, despair
New shoes, ripped pants, t-shirts, weird hair

A bike, a kiss and so many firsts
Giggles, laughs, shouts and outbursts

Often a thought how long will this last
So quickly reflecting how it went so fast

Congratulations, the kids are all grown, have moved out and you can settle into a life of simplicity, comfort and joy! They will never visit, never have grandchildren, won't request any kind of support, and you won't have any challenges visiting them during special occasions or holidays. Just start planning how you're going to spend all of your free time!

Yes, pretty easy to figure out that's not how it really goes. Even after the children move out, the blended family isn't over. It just takes a different form. You really don't have to solve everything to do with a blended family at once, so you if you want to put this book on the shelf for a few years, feel free. Come back to it when you're ready to face the next phase of topics dealing with a blended family. If you're ready right now, let's get started!

Post-high school living arrangements

For the sake of argument, let's assume that the vast majority of families consider it reasonable for the children to live in the blended family residence through high school. This section deals with the situations when the child(ren) may want or need to live in the blended family home after high school. It may be a matter of convenience, financial necessity, or just desire to continue living at home. You may also face a situation where a child wants to move back in after leaving for college or after some life event. It will be constructive to establish where both partners land on this topic in advance of facing the situation.

My opinion regarding allowing one or more of the children continuing to live at home after high school is:

	Partner A	Partner B
Not a chance, I don't support it		
Maybe, only if we can agree on a limited duration and other guidelines		
Maybe, let's discuss it and come up with a plan		
Yes, let's just outline a new set of expectations		
Yes, no concern at all		
I hope they live with us forever		
Other (explain)		

My opinion regarding allowing one or more of the children to move back into the home after moving out or finishing college:

	Partner A	Partner B
Not a chance, I don't support it		
Maybe, only if we can agree on a limited duration and other guidelines		
Maybe, let's discuss it and come up with a plan		
Yes, let's just outline a new set of expectations		
Yes, no concern at all		
Other		

My financial expectations if a grown child is going to move back in:

	Partner A	Partner B
They pay rent and carry an equal share of the house duties		
They must contribute financially and with duties but let's negotiate with the child		
Let's discuss what he/ she can afford and figure it out as we go		
No need to pay, but yes to house duties		
No need to pay or perform house duties		
Other (explain)		

HOSTING THE GROWN CHILD(REN) AND HIS/HER FAMILY

After the children move out, it can be a relief to both parents that any conflict present between each other and/or the children is now gone. The couple can focus on their relationship and spend more time and money on their own hobbies, entertainment and general enjoyment. Life just got quite a bit easier and quite a bit quieter. However, many parents find the "empty nest syndrome" to be very unsettling. While you may have looked forward to that peace, quiet, and free time, you may actually find yourself feeling a little lost and sad. The children's activities kept you busy and created a great deal of activity in the home. Now that's gone, both partners have to figure out how to fill those holes.

When the opportunity for the child(ren) to come back and visit presents itself, each parent may react differently. The parent that misses the child(ren) dearly may want frequent and extended visits: whereas, the other parent may want to keep the disruption to a minimum. Visits can cause the family to revive unresolved issues from the past and stir up topics that often caused conflict. It is helpful and productive for both partners to establish their stance on the various types of visits that might occur once the child(ren) move out.

My preference for handling visits from the grown child(ren) and his/her family is:

	Partner A	Partner B
I prefer the least number of visits possible		
A few visits per year is acceptable		
Open minded, but let's discuss and agree		
I'm agreeable to frequent visits as long as we have clear boundaries		
Let's have as many visits as possible		
Other (explain)		

My views on visits from grandchildren are:

	Partner A	Partner B
I'm not interested in the grandchildren visiting		
Visits must be scheduled, an agreed upon duration and we need to childproof the house		
Visits are ok but a limited duration is best		
Yes, visits are always welcome with a little advanced notice		
Absolutely, I want them to visit as much as possible		
Let's babysit the grandchildren often at their home or ours		
Other (explain)		

DOWNSIZING AND RETIRING

Now that the children are gone, couples often evaluate whether they need to maintain a large home. The rent/ mortgage cost, utilities and upkeep can be an undue financial burden and it can be taxing physically to keep the home in good condition. One partner may feel strongly that it's sensible or necessary to sell the home and downsize and the other partner may want to keep a home that is big enough to accommodate visits from the child(ren) and his/ her family.

The size of the home isn't the only major factor. It's very common for a couple approaching or at retirement to want to move to a more moderate or warm climate. Both partners need to find some agreement because moving to a warmer climate might mean moving away from the child(ren) and/or grandchildren. The relative importance of these big decisions needs to be explored.

My perspective on the house we should maintain after the child(ren) move out is:

	Partner A	Partner B
Move to a home that fits just us		
Downsize but still leave room for any visitors		
I'm flexible and don't have a strong opinion either way		
Stay or move, I want plenty of room for visitors		
I don't want to move at all		
Other (explain)		

My view of whether we should live near the child(ren) is:

	Partner A	Partner B
No, I don't want to live near the child(ren)		
Let's discuss it but I won't weight the location of the children very heavily		
Let's split time between a place we decide and a residence near the child(ren)		
Let's move away but we can visit frequently		
I want to live within a few hours of driving distance from the child(ren) and grandchild(ren)		
I won't move away from the child(ren) and grandchild(ren)		
Other (explain)		

FINANCIAL SUPPORT

Just because the child(ren) move out doesn't mean the financial support stops there. The child(ren) may run into financial issues at any stage of their adult life. It's very common for the child(ren) to continue to view one or both parents as an emotional and financial support system. It's helpful for both partners to get aligned on their views of providing financial support. As the couple approaches retirement age, money often becomes a much bigger concern and spending money on grown child(ren) has proven to be a contentious issue.

While we're at it, let's also just address the potential financial support needs of elderly parents. Having an elderly parent with an unexpected medical condition or in need of long-term care can create a significant unexpected financial burden. If the elderly parent needs support from one partner from the blended family, this can create significant stress on the relationship if the partners aren't aligned on how they want to support the parent.

My view of offering financial support to the grown child(ren) is:

	Partner A	Partner B
No way, not our responsibility		
Only in the case of emergency		
On a rare occasion I'd consider it		
I'm open to it but let's agree on the circumstances or criteria		
Sure, as long the money is paid back		
Yes, totally in favor of it but let's always discuss ahead of time		
Yes, anything they need is ok		
Other (explain)		

My view of offering financial support to the grandchild(ren) is:

	Partner A	Partner B
No way, not our responsibility		
Only in the case of emergency		
On a rare occasion I'd consider it		
I'm open to it but let's agree on what circumstances we would do it		
Sure, as long the money is paid back		
Yes, totally in favor of it but let's always discuss ahead of time		
Yes, anything they need is ok		
Other (explain)		

My perspective on paying for future grandchildren's post-secondary educational expenses is:

	Partner A	Partner B
No, not our responsibility		
Maybe under special circumstances		
I'd like to but not financially possible		
Offer a loan but not a gift		
Yes, a small amount would be nice		
Yes, as much as we can afford		
Other (explain)		

My view of spending money on gifts for birthdays and holidays for the grown child(ren) or grandchildren:

	Partner A	Partner B
No, not my thing		
No money or gifts but a card is appropriate		
Small gifts or money are appropriate		
Gifts or money for the big occasions but cards otherwise		
Always send a generous gift or money		
Other (explain)		

My view of financially supporting elderly parents is:

	Partner A	Partner B
Not our responsibility		
Only in the case of emergency and we must agree on the amount		
I'm open to it but let's discuss the circumstances		
Yes, definitely want to support the parents but let's agree on the terms		
Absolutely, whatever we need to do		
Other (explain)		

My view of whose responsibility it is to care for elderly parents is:

	Partner A	Partner B
Not our responsibility		
Maybe but rare circumstances		
Open to offering time but not money		
Willing to offer a little time and money but let's agree on terms		
Yes, let's offer whatever we can within reason		
Absolutely, whatever we need to do		
Other (explain)		

CHAPTER 6: ACTION PLAN

Agree, dissent, align or off track
I'm in it for me, no I've got your back

Happy, upset, thrilled, enraged
Miles apart or on the same page

Topics, logistics, decisions and rules
Guidance, agreements, practices and tools

All the topics our discussions did span
Nowhere we'll go without a good plan

If you've made it to this point, you have most likely had many healthy, productive discussions about your future blended family and you and your partner are contemplating what comes next. Maybe a few contentious discussions were sprinkled in there. Don't worry if you struggled a little while you were exploring challenging topics. Don't worry if you were unable to philosophically align on all key issues or you found that you need a little more work on a few skills. Very few couples, if any, will have glided through this process and finished without a healthy To Do list. Relationships are very hard work and we often overlook that they take a long-term, ongoing investment to make them successful. We're going to help you create a plan so there's structure and intention to move you forward. I know my personal tendency is to avoid scratching at contentious topics. An action plan is a good remedy for those who have the same inclination. You just need a little nudge, like I do, to keep these touchy topics front and center. You don't want to let unresolved issues linger or they move from inconveniences and irritations to battlegrounds and deal-breakers.

STEP 1 - MAKE A PRIORITIZED LIST

Let's start by making a list of skills or specific topics that you discussed that you both believe requires more work. You could call out two skills, communication and flexibility, and a few topics like household rules and dealing with the ex-spouses. Do your best to list them in order of priority but don't get bogged down.

Skills We Will Work On (In Order of Priority)

STEP 2 - NARROW YOUR FOCUS INITIALLY

If you identified multiple skills or topics you'd like to work on, that's fine. However, I recommend that you start with one skill and one topic so you don't get too overwhelmed trying to figure everything out at once. As the cliche' goes, you're better off going a mile deep on a few, than an inch deep on all of them. Relationships are a long-term investment, so you'll have time to get to the others. If you can build a good framework for learning and practicing with two, then you can continue that when you move on to others.

The first step I recommend is to spend time reflecting on where you think you'd like to grow with each skill you're focusing on. For example, if you selected compromise, write down several aspects of compromise that you do well and don't do well. Perhaps you wrote down that your initial reaction when faced with a compromise is to be rigid and inflexible. Then discuss that with your partner to get feedback. Perhaps your partner agrees with that one and added that you tend to want to win a disagreement rather than both achieve a mutually satisfying result.

Skill to Improve

Compromise

Topic to Address First

House rules

STEP 3 - CREATE AN ACTION PLAN

Pick the skill or topic you want to focus on first. Your options for investing in improving in this area could range from reading online articles, reading a book, speaking to a friend or mentor, practicing with your partner, or meeting with a counselor or expert to obtain advice and guidance. The key point is to understand that you need to offer commitment in the way of specific actions and a timeline. Otherwise, life tends to get in the way and these sorts of activities string along for months or never actually get addressed.

Partner A Action Plan

Action	Complete By
Read xyz article	*Sept 30*

Partner B Action Plan

Action	Complete By

STEP 4 - CIRCLE BACK

My recommendation is that you and your partner develop a routine where you each put time in each week/ couple of weeks and you have a time and/or place where you catch up on what you have each discovered and how that helps bring you closer to your blended family goals. You've chosen to focus on topics because you couldn't find agreement during your initial pass. Hopefully you've discovered new knowledge or insights that allow you both to reach agreement. If you need structure to describe what you learned and what your resolution was to the original disagreement, follow these guides below.

What I Learned

Agreement/ Resolution

STEP 5 - IF YOU ARE STUCK, GET HELP

If you find that your efforts aren't enough to help you improve in any particular area, enlist the help of a mentor, men's or women's group, church group, counselor, or therapist. Don't let ego or other superficial emotions get in the way of getting help. Communication, for example, is a very tricky skill to learn. We all have innate and learned habits when it comes to communicating. It takes time, investment, and patience to change ingrained habits. I have found workshops that both educate and allow for practice time are a really productive way to develop communication skills with your partner. I have also found that a counselor can help you and your partner understand different aspects of your communication style and challenge you to work on them. It almost goes without saying, counselors are an invaluable resource in overcoming challenges in a relationship.

STEP 6 - CELEBRATE PROGRESS

It is very important for you and your partner to acknowledge progress and celebrate wins along the way. Getting positive affirmation that you devoted energy to improving yourself and your relationship is a great motivator. Both of you should be positive and encouraging when steps are taken to help the blended family.

Resources

I want to emphasize several resources that might not be obvious to all readers. I have stressed online articles and books throughout this book and strongly advocated for using professionals in various disciplines. I also want to point out the abundance of information available in both audiobooks and podcasts. It is very common to see books published to hard copy, electronic and audio format these days. If reading a book or article isn't your thing, then look up the audio version. There are several smartphone apps that allow you to purchase the audio books or check them out for free just like a library book. OverDrive is the app I'm most familiar with for the latter purpose.

Podcasts are another very rich source of information. The popularity of podcasts continues to grow dramatically around the world as a source of information, entertainment and education. There are podcast shows that have very short episodes lasting 5-10 minutes and some that last several hours. Topics span across so many genres and subjects that it's difficult to summarize. Leave it to say you can find a podcast on just about any topic you can imagine. I have almost entirely replaced all the short gaps of time in my day with listening to inspirational or educational podcasts.

CHAPTER 7: MAYBE YOU SHOULDN'T BLEND

If the new team doesn't beam
The hype becomes a gripe

The happy gets more scrappy
The fun turns into glum

The talk becomes a balk
The law is now a flaw

If the blend doesn't mend
And the mix can no longer fix

Although it will ache
It may be time to break

One of the primary reasons I wrote this was to help prevent people from getting into an unpleasant blended family situation that has little chance for success. Breaking off a relationship or getting divorced a second or third time has the potential to be even more complicated and painful for you, your kids, and your family. If you and your partner go through this book and realize that your PA.W.S. isn't adding up, then don't do it. Spare yourselves, your children, your family, and your friends the hardship and expense. Breaking off any intimate relationship when cohabitation is involved will be complex. There's the emotional process one or both partners have to go through to decide to end the relationship. It can literally take years, in some cases, to come to the realization that the relationship won't work. Then you must figure out a plan to break it off and find a time and place to do it. The emotional part of the break-up is just the start!

After you've started the process to emotionally break up, then you have to figure out all the complex logistical challenges. Separating personal and household possessions, investments, finances, business ownership, healthcare plans, wills, and trusts are all potential big tasks to resolve. Then you factor in the impact to children involved. Changing living arrangements for children can be very unsettling and unpleasant. Young children, in particular, can be very impacted by moving to a new residence and losing a parent.

Next you consider the impact you, your partner, and the children have with family members. Parents and extended family members tend to pick the side of their biological family members. Relationships are broken when a blended family dissolves and the blended family members can become estranged. Finally, your blended family friends are affected as well. They could be drawn into the drama of the break-up and also become estranged from one or both partners and the children. There is usually a significant amount of collateral damage when families break up. This is the unseen 90% of the iceberg below the water, as the cliche goes, that you don't see as you're preparing to start your blended family.

Timing Isn't Right

Maybe after this book you decide that the relationship is still important but the timing isn't right to live together. After talking through all the practical considerations and understanding your PA.W.S., you decide that you need more time to work on the relationship before you add the complexity and pressure that can come with assimilating a blended family under the same roof. I recommend you continue to develop an action to help solve the PA.W.S. challenges you encountered while you're living apart. You may find that after you've invested in working through those challenges, timing will suit you much better at a later date. Keep working hard on your PA.W.S. and you'll be well suited for success!

Together but Separate

You might also realize that you want to continue your relationship but never blend the family in one household. I met someone who had an eight-year relationship that involved her raising and parenting her children in her home, while her partner lived in another home. He participated in family activities, but they never faced the challenges of coalescing parenting styles or agreeing on house rules. It was a completely non-confrontational situation for him because he could participate in family events, but not have the burden of being a stepparent.

Story: Katia was married for a second time about four years after her first marriage failed. She fell for Dmitry pretty fast because he was very handsome, shared many of the same interests in life and he was completely into her. He doted on her and wanted to be with her every minute. Within six months they were talking about moving in together, and he was undeterred by the fact that she had three young children under ten, even though he never had children. She thought that this period of living together would prove what kind of stepfather he would be to her children and would prove what kind of blended family relationship they would have. They had so much fun together as a couple and a family, shared deep love for each other, and seemed to have so many things required to make this second marriage successful. After four years of living together, getting married was a no-brainer to her. They were married in a beautiful ceremony and thought they were on a path to a lifetime of happiness. The shocking thing was that Dmitry changed very quickly after marriage. It seemed like a switch flipped and everything he had been holding back about his discomfort with living with her children just came flooding out. Out of the blue, their philosophical alignment about house rules and how to parent the kids became incredibly apparent. Dmitry became a tyrant about the simplest house rules. He expected the kids to comply to his rules without exception and he expected to be able to punish the children however and whenever he wanted. To Katia, he was overbearing and unnecessarily hard on the kids with every little move they made. She talked to him and pleaded with him to compromise and meet her terms on some issues. He just couldn't our wouldn't change. Over the course of the next two years, Katia and Dmitry's relationship suffered. The love they had was now full of resentment, anger and frustration. She wanted a home that was peaceful and loving and he wanted a home that was run how he was used to living. It took two more years of suffering, fighting and battling for Katia to realize she had to break things off. However, despite all the conflict, Dmitry didn't want to break up. Katia eventually had to file for divorce and endure an 18-month divorce that dragged her parents, friends and even the police into the situation. Katia was eventually free from Dmitry but still has lingering fears from the experience and several financial loose ends.

CHAPTER 8: THE BEGINNING, NOT THE END

Before you began, your odds were a glimmer
Identifying the challenges started the simmer

Assessing your will, got it quite warmer
Bad habits and poor communication are now former

Skills were sharpened and now you're getting hot
Resources and guidance give you a great shot

Soul-searching alignment then created the fire
Now your chances of success are such to admire

It would be a terrible idea to wrap up this book like a cold glass of reality splashed in your face. You've possibly had your hopes and dreams torn down like an NFL stadium from the '50s, so now it's time to build you back up. Blended families do work! Your future relationship doesn't have the same odds as the Minnesota Vikings winning the Super Bowl. (I'm a lifelong Vikings fan, I know pain.) Spend a few minutes and think about skills you developed over the course of your life that you consider yourself to be very good at. Maybe you've become a really good tennis player or are an excellent artist. Perhaps you've become very successful as an accountant or you are an expert project manager. All these things have one common denominator: it took education, practice, and determination to achieve your level of skill. Most people don't consider a relationship or a blended family to fall in the same category as playing tennis or being an accountant, but they should. You can learn, practice, and fine tune these blended family skills over time. It just takes commitment, effort, and perseverance (aka will.) Hopefully at this point you've learned that you can become very good at all the skills in this book. If you've made it to the end, the outlook for you and your partner to have a famously successful relationship should be excellent by now. You've just dramatically increased your awareness about what it takes to be successful and have plenty of pointers to help you continue to invest and grow. Today is a great day because you have so much to look forward to in your future blended family. Put in the love, time, and effort, and I know you'll be successful!

Made in the USA
Middletown, DE
17 April 2018